Start Before You're Ready

Praise for Jon Prince and *Start Before You're Ready*

'With deep empathy and hard-won wisdom, Jon helps people reconnect with their true selves, shift their mindset, and confidently create a life they genuinely love. Jon transforms mindsets and empowers people to live boldly, authentically, and free.'

Vex King, *Sunday Times* best-selling author of *Good Vibes, Good Life*

'Jon doesn't just inspire, he transforms the way you think. His powerful insights help you stop overthinking, take bold action, and create real momentum in your life.'

Hunter Fogarty, founder of Third Eye Thoughts

'Start Before You're Ready *is an inspired work! It will help you to turn procrastination into creativity and dreams into action. You will access a whole new level of inspiration and support if you follow Jon Prince's expert coaching and guidance. It's never too late to begin. Now is the time to say YES to living your higher purpose and do more of what you love.'*

Robert Holden, best-selling author of *Shift Happens!* and *Higher Purpose*

'Practical, powerful, and packed with truth. Start Before You're Ready *will shift how you see fear, failure, and yourself. If you've been stuck in self-doubt, read this and take the first step.'*

PETER SAGE, INTERNATIONAL SERIAL ENTREPRENEUR AND BEST-SELLING AUTHOR

'This is honestly some of the best stuff I have ever read. I didn't only learn something in every page, but it's also really clear and easy to understand and relate to. Jon has been a great support for me, helping me realign my thinking. His powerful and knowledgeable insights have been simple and clear and have led to more enjoyment and authenticity in my life and my career. I can't thank him enough.'

TRAVIS BOAK, AUSTRALIAN RULES FOOTBALLER

Start Before You're Ready

Stop Procrastinating, Overcome Fear and Take Control of Your Life

Jon Prince

HAY HOUSE

HAY HOUSE INDIA
New Delhi • London • Sydney
Carlsbad, California • New York City

Hay House Publishers (India) Pvt Ltd
Muskaan Complex, Plot No. 3, B-2, Vasant Kunj, New Delhi – 110070, India

Hay House LLC, P.O. Box 5100, Carlsbad, CA 92018-5100, USA
Hay House UK Ltd, 1st Floor, Crawford Corner, 91-93 Baker Street, London W1U 6QQ, UK
Hay House Australia Publishing Pty Ltd, 18/36 Ralph St., Alexandria NSW 2015, Australia

Email: contact@hayhouse.co.in
Website: www.hayhouse.co.in

The information given in this book should not be treated as a substitute for professional medical advice; always consult a medical practitioner. Any use of information in this book is at the reader's discretion and risk. Neither the author nor the publisher can be held responsible for any loss, claim, or damage arising out of the use, or misuse, of the suggestions made, the failure to take medical, advice or for any material on third-party websites.

First published by Hay House India, 2026
10 9 8 7 6 5 4 3 2 1

ISBN 978-93-6611-150-6

Printed at Repro India Limited

MIX
Paper from responsible sources
FSC® C047271
www.fsc.org

Hay House is committed to a sustainable future for our business, our readers and our planet. This book is made from Forest Stewardship Council® certified paper.

Mum and Dad, thank you for letting me walk my own path and find my own way in life, and for modeling love, kindness, and commitment.

My wife, Michelle, I love you – thank you for loving me unconditionally, always believing in me, and for your support while I worked on this book.

To my children, you are both my daily inspiration and my greatest teachers.

Finally, this book is for each of you who's brave enough to make your dreams more important than your fears.

Contents

Introduction

For a long time, I wanted to write a book. I love writing, but I couldn't get started. Why not? The truth is, I didn't know where to start. I was scared. What if what I wrote wasn't good enough? What if my book got compared to the great writers who have come before me? If there are already books out there on these topics, why should I write another one? Who am I to write a book anyway? Would I need more experience before I could start? The doubts kept on coming. I could have stayed in my head thinking about all the reasons and excuses why I shouldn't write this book, but, fortunately, that's not what happened.

Self-doubt, overthinking, and perfectionism will rise anytime you decide to do something that's important to you. You may start to question yourself and your abilities, you might compare yourself to others, and you may find yourself taking on other tasks as a distraction, like tidying the house. All of this keeps you waiting until you feel ready.

But what I'm going to show you in this book is that waiting to feel ready is a trap. Not feeling ready is the uncomfortable feeling that holds you back and prevents you from taking action. It's the mind's way of clinging on to the familiar – your past experiences, identity, comfort zones, and the illusion of control. It whispers, 'Wait until it's perfect, safe, or certain,' keeping you stuck in fear and indecision. Here's the truth: 'Ready' is an illusion. You'll never feel completely ready because growth demands stepping into the unknown. It's supposed to feel uncomfortable and uncertain, and those feelings are a sign that you're breaking free from what's been holding you back. Waiting to feel ready only delays the very growth and transformation you crave and keeps your fears and limiting patterns alive. This is why the procrastinator puts off starting the course or hiring a coach, which are the very resources that could help them break free. It's why the person who wants to network waits for confidence before stepping into a room and introducing themselves to people, even though doing that would give them the confidence they long for. And it's the reason the person who is overwhelmed feels too busy to take a break, which is the very thing that would help them gain the clarity they desperately desire.

It's time to break free from the old paradigms and shift your perceptions about who you are, what 'works,' and what's possible for you. The magic happens when you take the counterintuitive steps to start before you're ready. That's where your real power and potential lie – and this book will show you how to take that leap.

Maybe you want to start a new business, launch a podcast, quit an unsatisfying job, start dating, commit to a fitness plan, believe in yourself, or write your first book. The chapters that follow will help you get into action by showing you how to follow your curiosity instead of being guided by your fears.

A Bit About Me

I was five years into a nine-year career as a professional poker player when I hit rock bottom. I had no success in romance, I had lost all belief in myself, and I had no purpose. On the outside, I was living my dream, even playing poker in the World Series of Poker Main Event, which I'd dreamed of doing since watching it on TV when I was younger, but life was not so good on the inside. While playing poker and gambling thousands of dollars each day, I suffered with overthinking, overwhelm, and stress. Poker required me to face the unknown and uncertainty, and my unwillingness to surrender to it led to anxiety and self-doubt. I chased the next win or the next high in the hope that it would bring me the inner peace, fulfillment, and security I so deeply craved. I waited for a magic bullet to come along and bring me confidence, but it never arrived.

Then, I experienced an inner shift. I stopped looking outward for the answers and instead turned my focus inward. I discovered it wasn't the world of poker that was creating my problems – it was my perceptions. The day it clicked was the day I realized that I am not my thoughts. All the inner chaos I was experiencing was coming from believing my thoughts to be true. I saw that I get to choose what things mean in life, and when I was no longer attached to my thoughts, I could create my reality. Fear was no longer something to run from; it was the very place I needed to move toward. I discovered a new me, one I never knew existed, and I got into action like never before. Life became exciting and took on a whole new meaning.

Over the next year, I quit poker, stopped just reading books and watching YouTube videos without putting the teachings into practice, and expanded my comfort zone by taking inspired actions led by my heart and not my head. I built my confidence day by day by trying new things, like cooking different recipes, taking improv comedy classes, and engaging in public speaking, but I still lacked something. These activities were exciting and fun, but I craved connection, contribution, and purpose. Then I discovered a charity called The Listening Place that supports people who are suicidal by giving them a safe and confidential space to share their story. Having developed a passion for mindset and mental well-being, I applied to work there and, after completing my training, was taken on as a listening volunteer.

I grew immensely during this time, being around such kind souls and having the privilege to support some of the bravest people you could ever meet. My role was to listen to the 'visitors,' without giving them any advice, and allow them to be seen, heard, and valued. A few weeks into my time there, I experienced a moment that changed everything when a visitor told me about the traumas, challenges, and battles they'd faced. I thought they were one of the most courageous people I'd ever met. They shared something that hit me hard – they said, 'I don't deserve to be here.' I'd often felt unworthy, not good enough, or like a fraud, but to hear someone say they didn't feel worthy of being here, on this planet, put everything into perspective. Everyone deserves the chance to be loved and to love themselves, and I refused to sit by and watch others believe a lie that hurt them so deeply. I had found my purpose, a cause greater than myself. My mission became to help people love who they are and find meaning in what they do through altering their perceptions. I had experienced profound shifts in myself and now it was time to learn the tools to help others make these changes too.

Over the next few years, I learned about and practiced many of the tools I'll be offering you in this book. I worked with therapists and coaches and took courses. I studied philosophy and practiced meditation and mindfulness daily. I gained a Masters in Psychology, but, most importantly, I put all that I'd learned into practice by facing my fears out in the real world, making mistakes and learning from each of them.

I wanted the world to know what I knew about mindset and how it can change your life and the way you feel about yourself, so I set myself up as The Perception Coach on Instagram and shared what I'd learned in the hope that it would help just one person. Seven years later and I've amassed over 180,000 followers across my social media pages, and my videos have been viewed by millions of people. I've achieved a Diploma in Transformational Coaching, a certification in Bradian Hypnotherapy, set up my own coaching business, and worked with hundreds of clients from all walks of life, from business owners, CEOs, top athletes, teachers, and students, to coaches, physiotherapists, and high-roller poker players.

Having worked with people from all around the world, I see so many of the same blocks coming up again and again in different guises. My role as a coach is to empower people and my mission is to help them gain the tools they need to succeed, to achieve mental and emotional freedom, and live a life of purpose and meaning. There's no greater tool than the wisdom you have inside you, and it's my intention with this book to help you unlock that. While one-to-one work is powerful,

I know it's not available to everyone and that some lessons take time to learn and are most effective when presented in the pages of a book for regular reflection. I was motivated to write this book so that all of you can access the ideas, strategies, and mindset shifts required to change your life.

I've always loved reading personal development books and listening to audios from the greats, such as Dr. Wayne Dyer, Tony Robbins, Brené Brown, Susan Jeffers, Albert Ellis, and Eckhart Tolle. Their books had such a positive influence and gave me the tools I needed to educate myself and keep going when I wanted to give up. It's been a dream of mine to share my unique perspective and impact others in the same way they impacted me, and it's an honor to share this book with you. I won't be suggesting anything in these pages that I either haven't done myself or wouldn't do. Trust me, they all work.

How to Use This Book

Start Before You're Ready is a manual for understanding yourself and getting into action. In the chapters that follow, we'll tackle and dismantle each of the mental obstacles that block you from taking action – from procrastination, overthinking, and indecision to self-doubt, fear, and impostor syndrome. You'll discover the power of letting go of the need for certainty and be inspired to take imperfect action by starting badly.

I believe that personal growth should be fun and enjoyable, so I present the tools, secrets, and strategies I've learned over the years in a way that's practical and relatable. As you work through the chapters, you may find one tool that resonates with you more than others and, if that's the case, run with it and use it. What works for one person in one moment will be different for others in another moment. There's not one right way to be confident or to be you; you'll find your own way. And when you find your true self, you'll also find the courage and self-confidence to release your inner wisdom.

I recommend reading the book from cover to cover, because each of the concepts helps unlock the others. As you understand impostor syndrome, for example, you'll procrastinate less and, as you procrastinate less, you'll become more confident. The chapters work together to give you a complete tool kit to start before you're ready and step into unconditional self-acceptance. Once you've read through the whole book, you can always dip into any of the chapters you need in a particular moment. This book can serve as a reference manual to help you overcome any mind-made obstacles and get back into inspired action.

The most important thing I've learned from over 10 years of studying personal development is that what's in the personal development books works, but you have to apply what you learn. I spent years just consuming knowledge with nothing changing until, one evening, I read a Tony Robbins book, got out my pen and paper, wrote down my goals, and decided to take action on them. The rest, as they say, is history. Throughout the book, I've therefore included short exercises for you to complete to help you put into practice what you've learned and turn insight into reality. I recommend either reading the book through and then coming back to do the exercises afterward, or pausing to take them on whenever you feel inspired. You don't have to do them all, but you do need to take action to get the full benefits of this book. Catch the times when you find yourself wanting to wait to take action later and see these as triggers to do one or more of the exercises. You'll find that your first step leads to your next, and each step gives you the courage to keep taking action. I've also included key takeaways at the end of each chapter to really cement the lessons, as well as a 'lens check' at the start and end of each chapter to give you an experience of what it's like to see the world through the problem and then how it feels to see it from a new perspective. As you gather the tools in this book, you'll change your lens and see the world with new eyes.

I learned about starting before you're ready by doing it and being it. I then had to go back through that journey while writing this book. I used all the tools I share with you here to help me start, keep going, and present something I'm immensely proud of. This book will help you give yourself permission to embrace the discomfort, take risks, and start now. Whatever domain of life you're in, the tools will help you to overcome your inner obstacles and create your version of success so you can live with confidence, inner peace, and clarity.

An important disclaimer before we dive in: Starting before you're ready is something you get to spend a lifetime mastering. You may experience instant shifts in energy, excitement, and passion, but, like working out in the gym, it's something you need to keep practicing and living every day to keep experiencing. Starting before you're ready is a mindset shift and, even beyond that, it's a reality shift. It's the ability to be creative in every moment, to trust yourself and be willing to fail on the journey to success. It's knowing that you won't always feel ready when stepping into the unknown, and it's turning the stop sign into a go sign.

If you're willing to open your mind to new perspectives and let go of the need for permanence, certainty, and comfort, your world will shift. I'll be walking alongside you every step of the way. Let's go.

CHAPTER 1

Stop Being a Perfectionist

So many people think that you need confidence to start something, but I'm here to tell you that's a myth. The first step to starting before you're ready is being willing to start badly. You might be thinking to yourself, *Why on Earth would I want to start badly? Why would I want to fail? That makes no sense to me!* The first time you try anything new, you might succeed straight off the bat and, if you do, that's fantastic, but in reality it's likely you'll make some mistakes and experience some failures – and you need to get comfortable with that.

Everyone wants to start off as an expert, but we need to start as a beginner. A beginner's mindset of curiosity and wonder allows us to absorb information and insights that might get missed when we think we already have the answers. Avoiding this is avoiding reality, which creates unnecessary suffering. So many of us want to get things right first time – we need a guarantee of success, we want to avoid making mistakes or making a fool of ourselves – and it's at this point that perfectionism shows up.

When perfectionism is at play, you might find yourself putting off making decisions or waiting instead of taking action. You might convince yourself you need more qualifications or confidence before taking the leap. Perhaps you find yourself spending hours searching for the right way of doing something, or you may feel you need to have everything fully prepared before you take your first step. You'll often feel worried and panicked that you might fail. All these strategies, including worry, are an attempt to control the outcome and avoid the feelings of doubt, uncertainty, stress, or discomfort that arise when you step into the unknown.

Perfectionism is 'self'-protection – its goal is to make sure you get it right first time so that you never experience failure. It's protecting you from being judged or looking bad. At the root of perfectionism lies the fear of not being good enough (we'll look closely at how to resolve this in Chapter 9). The problem is that self-protection can lead to self-rejection, where you place avoiding fear and trying to look good above your own needs, desires, goals, and values.

The perfectionist in you strives for flawlessness and sets standards so high they're almost impossible to reach. The work you do is either perfect or a failure, where 9/10 is short of success and only 10/10 will do. This can lead to excessive and harsh self-criticism, stress, and feelings of inadequacy. Perfectionism is a learned strategy designed to make you feel comfortable, safe, and gain a sense of control, but the truth is, it does the opposite. Consider that perfection is a mirage – it's a destination you'll never reach, and because it's always just out of reach, you live in the world of never feeling ready or in control. The pursuit of perfection keeps you stuck in place as you wait for perfect conditions before acting.

> ### LENS CHECK
>
> Take a moment to reflect on what life is like for someone who needs everything to be absolutely perfect. Imagine how tense they feel in their body and the stress they experience thinking about future projects. What must it feel like to always be chasing something that's unattainable, constantly reaching for the unreachable? How do they feel about themselves and about life? What are tasks like for them? How much do they get done? Picture how serious life is when everything has to be perfect and how heavy the load feels when every step is weighed down by the pursuit of perfection.

Having the ability to not feel ready and still take action is a superpower, and it's this very feeling that I'll show you how to master, manage, and transcend. I invite you to get used to not feeling ready, to embrace uncertainty, and be open to changing how you respond to this feeling. If you do, you'll be able to access your inner confidence whenever you need it. If you don't, you may spend your whole life searching for the magic bullet.

Quit Chasing the Magic Bullet

Waiting to feel ready is like waiting for a magic bullet. I define the magic bullet as a product, person, or process that you believe will come along and take away all your problems forever. It's every marketer's dream: It's what they sell us all on. *When I have this next product, I can escape failing forever. When I have this one skill, I'll never have to feel doubt or fear again. When I get the five-step blueprint, I'll be complete.* As you saw in the Introduction, I spent years chasing the allure of the magic bullet, hoping it would bring me confidence, until I learned that, as long as you're growing, you can't escape failure, doubt, and uncertainty. Trying to make these go away is the problem. Even if you have all the success in the world, there'll always be new challenges you might fail at and uncharted areas of your life to navigate. If we can't escape these feelings, we must therefore surrender to them.

Surrendering doesn't mean giving up; it means choosing to accept what you can't control and focusing on what you can. A gladiator surrenders to the possibility of his death when he walks into the arena and, by no longer trying to avoid death, he can play full out. When you no longer try to avoid failing, you can play to win. When you no longer try to avoid uncertainty, you'll feel more confident. When you no longer try to get rid of doubt, you can make empowered decisions – this is freedom.

The real magic bullet is to give up needing one and to know that you can fail, experience doubt, feel uncertainty, and still be confident and complete. When you stop searching for the magic bullet and waiting for the uncomfortable feelings to go away, you'll see that *you* are the magic bullet, and you have the power to transform your fears and feelings into success. So, stop waiting for the perfect time or conditions, stop waiting for confidence, and stop waiting to do it right – instead, embrace the art of starting badly.

Start Badly

'Anything that's worth doing is worth doing badly.'

– Unknown

The first time you give a speech, it will likely suck. The first time you go on a date, you will likely fumble your words or be nervous. The first time you dive into a swimming pool, you will likely belly flop. And yet what do we say to ourselves when trying a new skill, taking on a new project or task, or making decisions? The mantra that enters our mind is one of the following: 'I have to do it perfectly,' 'I'd better get it right,' or 'I must not fail.'

Most of us can't stand the idea of failing, so we avoid it at all costs. We replace the possibility of failing with an insistence on achieving our desired outcome, hence the mantra, 'I must succeed!' The result of this is unnecessary expectation and pressure, which manifests itself as fear. The fear shows up as the fear of failure, the fear of rejection, and the fear of embarrassment. These fears consume us so deeply that we assume we must start perfectly so we don't have to experience them.

**You have a choice:
inspired action or perfectionism.**

There are two ways you can approach new challenges: You can strive to do your best, start badly, and learn as you go. Or you can study everything about it, figure it all out, make sure you have everything just right because this is your only shot at it, and then – and only then, when you're 100 percent sure that you'll succeed – dip your toe in and get started. The first strives for success and the second aims to avoid failure.

Which category do you fall into? Getting in there and figuring it out as you go along and striving for success, or playing it safe to avoid failing? Now consider that this can also show up in different areas of your life. You might be great at diving head-first into challenges at work, but then you're cautious and perfectionistic when it comes to your relationships. Perhaps you're great at reaching out to friends, but stuck when it comes to introducing yourself to new people, wanting to find the perfect thing to say. Some of us are perfectionists about specific things and others are perfectionists about everything.

I share these two categories with you because I fell firmly into the second one – I would do everything perfectly or not at all. I was a perfectionist in almost every area of my life. When cooking, I would follow the recipe down to the very last ounce of flour; I would film 20 takes of a video before putting it out on social media to make sure it was flawless; I expected in my first coaching session to be like Tony Robbins, curing someone of all their life's problems in just 60 minutes; and I would spend weeks perfecting a workshop before delivering it to a group of participants. That was until I discovered what I'm going to share with you in this chapter, and then I experienced freedom, authenticity, and confidence – and you will too.

If you always succeed at everything you do, then it's likely you fall into the 'playing it safe' category. This isn't bad or wrong, but it means that you'll be operating at about 20 percent of your full potential because you're slowed down by trying to start perfectly. Windy Dryden, one of the world's highest regarded therapists and trainers, said, 'If you haven't made any mistakes lately, you're either dead or playing things extraordinarily safe.' If you have the feeling that you have a great deal of potential but you just can't access it, stick with me and stay open to the possibility of starting badly, letting go of what holds you back, and reclaiming your mental and emotional freedom.

Preparation is an important part of success, but when you try to prepare perfectly, you set yourself up for a life of anxiety, panic, and stress and, unfortunately, the success that you're running toward will run away from you. Life becomes one big preparation where you never feel ready. Even if you do experience some success, it will only give you a temporary sense of relief before the next project starts and the anxiety returns. Uncomfortable feelings are not always a sign you're in the wrong place and need to run; they show up when you're breaking old patterns, leaning into your edge, and upgrading your perspective. Doubt and fear often arise just as you're on the verge of stepping outside your comfort zone, and discomfort is a sign you're growing.

Starting badly is your own internal permission slip to be ready right now instead of having to wait to get ready. It's making the choice of short-term discomfort for long-term improvement and well-being. It's doing what you love instead of being driven by fear. It will get you into action, into motion, off the sidelines, and onto the pitch.

The first step to starting badly is to lower the bar for success. Instead of trying to start perfectly, give yourself permission to reduce your standards for starting and get into action faster – there's plenty of time for you to get great later. Change the way you see failure – it doesn't have to be your enemy; you can make it your friend.

Mistakes Are the Best Way to Learn

Your mistakes are some of the best learning tools you'll ever have access to – after all, if you get it right first time there's nothing you can learn from the experience. Failure can be your friend if you get to know it, understand it, and don't run from it. You're meant to stumble a little the first time you do something – and you'll experience unnecessary suffering when you try to escape this. When you strive to be perfect right away, your expectations about how amazing things should be from the start restrict your natural curiosity and ability to experiment, which are essential to taking action. It's like expecting a child to walk the moment they have the desire to do so. Children are master speed-learners because they're messy, they experiment, and they learn by doing, failing, and trying again. They aren't self-conscious, they don't stop to think about how they look, and they'll do it naked in front of everyone if necessary. They're entirely immersed in what they are doing.

There's a time to perfect things and focus on the details, but this isn't at the start. If you want to master anything, you need to master failing fast and failing often. This way, mistakes become something you're used to, not something you avoid like the plague. If you always succeed at everything you do, then failure will be alien to you – we fear the unknown, which makes failure even scarier.

I think of perfectionism as the person who wants to turn on the light but doesn't want to experience the inconvenience and discomfort of getting up from their seat and crossing the room to do so. Instead, they decide to craft a device that will enable them to turn on the light from where they're sitting without having to move. They spend hours tying together items within reach and, eventually, they have a perfectly crafted stick that turns on the light. The problem is, they fail to notice that it took them hours to do something they could have done in a fraction of the time if they were willing to lean into the temporary discomfort of getting up and walking across the room. This perfectly illustrates how perfectionism is the illusion of having a shortcut to avoid inconvenience, discomfort, and effort but actually results in more inconvenience, discomfort, and effort. You can't escape inconvenience and, if you're playing life full out, you can't avoid failure and making mistakes. The paradox is that when you choose to embrace them, life becomes more convenient and you'll become an inspired action-taker. You don't wait, you don't hesitate, you simply get up and turn on the light.

If you think you might fail, that's the direction to move in. When you live as if it's OK to fail, you are free.

There are opportunities waiting all around you right now if you're willing to take steps forward. Take the thing you want to do now or the project you want to start and, instead of thinking of it as potentially being a success or failure, ask yourself, 'What can I learn from starting? What steps do I need to take?' Would a mistake in one area mean the whole thing is a failure or would it give you valuable feedback to improve? Will this be the only project you'll ever start, or will there be more?

Break the Rules

The perfectionistic demands you place on yourself are expectations in the form of 'musts,' 'shoulds,' and 'have-tos.' I learned about many of these internal demands from the work of psychologist Albert Ellis. These unconscious, self-imposed rules make starting a challenge. Here are some examples:

- 'I have to succeed.'
- 'I must not fail.'
- 'Other people must like what I do.'
- 'I should do perfectly well.'
- 'I must not make any mistakes.'
- 'I should do it without effort.'
- 'It should be easy.'
- 'I must not experience any inconvenience.'

You subconsciously took on many of these rules from influential people throughout your formative years – demanding parents, teachers, or role models who told you that you must perform well. Now you can make a conscious choice to drop them. Such rules are inflexible and create rigid thinking. The internal demands you place on yourself create pressure, anxiety, and stress, which we'll dismantle further in Chapter 6. If you don't want to live with the rule that you 'should always succeed' or you 'must never fail,' you don't have to. You get to choose the personal rules you live by. When you change your thinking from 'I have to get it right' to 'I want to get it right, but I don't have to,' something magical occurs – you give yourself permission to fail.

EXERCISE

Write down the unconscious rules you have around starting and taking action; all the 'musts,' 'shoulds,' and 'have-tos.' Then answer the following questions: 'Who says you must? Where did these demands come from? Did you make them up or did someone teach them to you or project them on to you? How do these rules hold you back? How do you feel when you follow them?' Consciously choose to give up the ones that no longer serve you and instead create standards that are more flexible and aligned with what you want. For example, 'I must succeed' could become 'I will try my best.' This is much more fun and freeing, and will allow you to perform without pressure.

Take one of the rules you no longer want and spend the next week breaking it (you'll get a chance to practice this later in the chapter).

Wanting to succeed but not having to is more about preference than pressure – you choose it. Success is driven by your internal desires and conscious choices rather than external expectations. This allows for greater freedom, flexibility, and enjoyment.

Break the Spell of Black-and-White Thinking

The reason we have a problem with perfectionism and starting badly is because we have a problem with the idea of 'bad' itself. This comes from a cognitive distortion all humans experience called black-and-white thinking, also known as all-or-nothing thinking. This distortion in thinking arises when we perceive situations in absolute terms without considering the complexities of them, and it leads to generalizations and blowing things out of proportion. It's seeing something as black and white without acknowledging the gray in between.

Some examples of black-or-white thinking include:

- 'If I don't get a perfect score on this exam, I'm a failure.'
- 'Either you're with me or you're against me.'
- 'I always mess things up. I can never do anything right.'
- 'If I'm not the best at something then I'm the worst at it.'
- 'It didn't go exactly as I planned; therefore, it's a complete disaster.'
- 'I'm either a beginner or an expert.'
- 'I'm going to do it perfectly or not at all.'
- 'If I miss a day then I might as well give up.'

Each of the above examples is more complex than simply one or the other. Thinking of not getting a perfect exam score as a complete failure misses the fact that you might have had an off day, and failing one exam doesn't mean you're a failure as a person. In 2016, Lionel Messi missed a penalty in the Copa América final against Chile, and Argentina went on to lose the match. After the match, Messi announced his retirement from international football – maybe a little all-or-nothing thinking crept into his mind. He soon reversed this decision and went on to lift the World Cup trophy six years later. Messi was the first to step up and score in the penalty shootout, leading his country to World Cup glory. At the time of writing, Messi has taken 141 penalties in open play, scoring 110 and missing 31. That's a 78 percent – not a 100 percent – success rate. Lionel Messi can miss a penalty, even in a final, and still be, without doubt, one of the best football players of all time.

If you adopt all-or-nothing thinking around success and failure, it can make starting feel like a scary prospect. Yet, when you see failure as a natural part of the success cycle, like a wave crashing and rising again, you can embrace it as part of the journey.

Let's take another example from the list above: thinking that if you miss a day you should give up. This all-or-nothing thinking causes you to miss the fact that one skipped day doesn't mean you've failed. One missed workout session or morning sleeping in too late doesn't mean you have to give up all together. This way of thinking makes new tasks feel daunting. You might feel like you have to read a whole book cover to cover, or it's not worth reading at all. You may want to be the best in the world at the new venture you're considering starting, otherwise you won't even bother. Instead of all-or-nothing thinking, consider *all-in* thinking where you stay all-in on your goal without having to do it perfectly each day. If you miss a day or mess up, you keep going. This gives you room to misstep and still stay on the path. It will help you take more action and be more consistent. Twenty-four days out of 30 is better than 10 days in a row and then quitting. Doing a little of something each day over months is better than trying to do it all in a day and burning out before you've even begun.

Anytime you notice the words 'always' or 'never' cropping up in your thoughts, you have drifted into all-or-nothing thinking. Our brain naturally judges. If we had to process all the complexities of every situation, it would be exhausting. So, instead, our brain automatically places people and situations into categories by taking mental shortcuts. It thinks 'always' and 'never' instead of 'sometimes.' It says 'good' or 'bad' instead of 'complex.' The paradox is, when our brain tries to simplify, it can make our lives more complex. Unfortunately for you and me, this means seeing ourselves as a failure or not good enough when we make a mistake – a big part of perfectionism and what leads to the third thought in the list above: 'I can never do anything right.'

If you have a core belief that you're not good enough or you're a failure, any mistake or criticism might trigger this, and you'll seek to confirm this belief through the lens of 'If I'm not the very best then I'm not good enough.' The problem with this all-or-nothing polarizing way of thinking is it leads to swing confidence: When you succeed you feel amazing and when you fail you feel awful. I caught it myself as I was writing this chapter – I noticed myself feeling great when I nailed a paragraph that felt right and then I started to doubt my writing abilities when I hit a roadblock.

Here's the thing: Black-and-white thinking isn't a problem when you know you're doing it, which is why I'm still enjoying the process and maintaining my confidence levels as I write; I'm observing my thoughts and not buying into them. I can find a section of writing challenging, I can hit a roadblock, and I can get lost, yet I can still be on the road to success. If you fail an exam and catch yourself thinking, *This means I'm a failure*, pause it right there and ask yourself, 'Where else have I succeeded? What questions did I do well on?' If you find yourself thinking, *I never get things right*, break it down: Do you 'always' mess things up or have there been times when you've succeeded? If you feel the need to do something all at once or not at all, consider what it would be like to take that pressure off.

EXERCISE

Where do you think in terms of black and white? Where in your life does this kind of thinking show up for you? Are there people, situations, and places where you think in all-or-nothing terms? Does it help or hurt? How does it stop you from starting? Consider how much freedom comes from knowing you can choose to think in a more balanced way.

Your brain also seeks to confirm past beliefs to make sense of the world and create a sense of certainty. If you make a mistake and start to think that you never do anything right, you'll look for all the times you've failed and discount all your successes. Messi could have stayed retired after the Cup Final loss and never had his hands on the World Cup trophy. When you break the spell of black-and-white thinking, you make failure without fear a real possibility because you know it doesn't have to mean the end. Instead, failure is simply a dent in the road, and the road can still be one worth traveling on.

When you allow yourself to get a little messy, make some mistakes, and experiment in the gray zone a little more, you'll feel freer. Success and failure, perfect and useless, good and bad - these are all too absolute and, in fact, all two sides of the same coin. You can't have success without failure; you can't have perfection without imperfection; and you can't have good without bad. Trying to start perfectly is avoiding many of life's necessary elements. Black-or-white thinking isn't the problem; it's when we lack awareness that it's happening and then make decisions about ourselves and others from this place that it becomes a problem. Awareness is one of your greatest gifts. Keep this in mind as we continue this journey together over the following pages.

Zoom out

All-or-nothing thinking creates a distortion in your perceptions. However, with awareness, this distortion doesn't need to drive your actions.

Let me give you an example. Black-or-white thinking is like saying if your T-shirt has a mark on it, the T-shirt is useless, or if you have a pimple on your face, that means you're ugly. Or if you have one doubting thought, it means you lack confidence. Or if a server forgot your drink order, the whole service was terrible. It means taking one tiny detail and making it into a massive problem. It changes how you feel altogether. When you focus on the black mark or the pimple, you forget that the rest of you – or someone else for that matter – is working fine! The more you focus on something, the more of it you get. When you focus on the black mark, you feel bad; when you focus on the drink the server forgot, you miss the fact that they smiled, asked how your day was, brought the food out on time, or that they are another human being with imperfections just like you. All-or-nothing thinking means you're either perfect or a failure, and when you let this go, you can get started more often with more freedom.

To overcome all-or-nothing thinking, zoom out and put the thinking into its proper place. If you had a setback, look at the whole performance. Did you have any successes? If you delivered a presentation and forgot a line and fumbled some of your words, did you still deliver some value? Will others learn something from your presentation? Were you courageous for standing up and speaking? Did you gain some experience? Was it still a success? Are *you* still a success?

Also notice where in your life you judge others in an all-or-nothing way, as either good or bad, success or failure. It will teach you so much about yourself. If you're doing this to others, you're doing this to yourself. If you think someone's performance is a failure because they made one mistake, you'll give yourself the same black-and-white treatment, making it harder for you to embrace failure. The less you judge others as a whole and in all-or-nothing terms, the less you will judge yourself. You can practice this everywhere and bring it to the tasks and projects you want to start. When you see others fail yet take note of the courage and success within the faults, it will make failure less scary for you.

It's Time to Become an Experimenter

No more waiting – by now, you've seen that starting before you're ready requires a willingness to embrace some mistakes, discomfort, and failure. By choosing to surrender to this, you can and will become an inspired action-taker, and overcome perfectionism and your fear of mistakes. Now it's time for the next step in starting badly: putting on your metaphorical lab coat and experimenting.

My question for you is: Are you ready to dip your toe in or dive in at the deep end? Both are great options because they involve taking action; it just depends on what stage you're at along your journey and how fast you want to progress. Consider the toe dip as the beginner level and the deep end as the advanced. The goal with either of these challenges is to experiment – it's not a test for you to succeed or fail at; it's a learning experience.

Dipping your toe in = starting something new

The first option is to dip your toe in. If this is your preference, consider something you've been putting off for too long and simply take the first step. You might fail, you might succeed, but your goal is to be an experimenter. You're simply testing things out to see what happens. You might make a mistake, you might not. You might feel embarrassed, you might not. Either way, you'll be stepping into the unknown, where transformation and growth happen.

Here are some options for you to choose from:

- Cook a meal you've never cooked before.
- Take up a new class or hobby.
- Send an email you've been putting off.
- Get messy: Go to the beach and get sand on yourself; dance in the rain and get wet; or have a food fight with yourself or a friend and embrace the mess.
- Reply to a message instantly when you would usually put it off.
- Write the first page of your new book.
- Invite a friend out.

Diving in at the deep end = trying to fail on purpose

You can go straight to this challenge or warm up by dipping your toe in first. If you're ready to dive in at the deep end, then it's time to fail on purpose. Practice failing, seek it, go after it; stop trying to do things perfectly and start badly. Success cannot exist without failure; for you to be free psychologically and emotionally, you must experience both. What you run from will chase you your whole life, so shift your perspective around failure, mistakes, embarrassment, and disappointment. When you run right at failure, you'll overcome your fear of it as you see that it's just an illusion.

As Alan Watts says, 'Whenever confronted with a ghost, walk straight into it and it will disappear.' Your fears are ghosts and so are the ideas of failure, mistakes, and getting it wrong. They are all thought-created judgments. When you fail, you'll no longer be afraid of failing. This is diving in at the deep end.

Here are some options for you to choose from:

- Mispronounce a word you know in conversation and keep talking as usual.
- Raise your hand in a group situation, like a meet-up or a workshop, and ask a silly question.
- Pitch an idea to someone that you know might fail.
- Go to work, the gym, or a social occasion without doing your hair.
- Share a time you failed with someone you trust.
- Play a sport you've never tried before.
- Risk getting a 'no' from a potential date or new client.
- Leave a typo in an email or social media or blog post on purpose.

Feel free to get creative and think of your own. The key here is to fail, feel the feelings, and know it means nothing about you or your ability to succeed. Prove to yourself that you can fail in the short term and succeed in the long run.

I suggest putting this book down and taking one of these actions at your earliest convenience – the sooner the better. Remember, you won't feel ready to do it; that's the whole point. Start before you're ready! This is a book of action, a book of transformation, and there will be plenty more chances for you to step out of your comfort zone as we work through the following chapters. Like driving a car, you get the experience for yourself from doing it, not just thinking about it.

> ## LENS CHECK
>
> Take a moment to reflect on what life is like for someone who strives for excellence but doesn't need things to be perfect. They do their best and let go of having to control the outcome, knowing that their goal is to improve, have fun, and enjoy what they are doing. How do they feel about life? How much lighter and freer are they without the weight of perfection on their shoulders? What are tasks like for them? How much do they get done?

I hope you now understand that you don't have to start perfectly. Perfection is the result of many imperfect parts coming together over time to form something great. Life is an experiment, not a test of your worth. It's a place where you get to try out new things and learn by doing, not by waiting around and trying to perfect it first. Get into action quickly and see failure as part of the process; when you make a mess, you learn to grow by cleaning it up. Failure can be your biggest ally and provide you with valuable feedback to grow. See the bigger picture, look for the gray, and break free from the restraints of perfection.

Next, we're going to tackle something I see a lot of my clients struggling with – overcoming indecision.

KEY TAKEAWAYS

- **Stop looking for the magic bullet and, instead, get into action by starting now.**
- **Notice where you experience black-and-white thinking and look for the gray.**
- **Drop the need to start perfectly by taking on a challenge or risk; fail on purpose and step out of your comfort zone.**

CHAPTER 2

Overcome Indecision

We're all faced with so many decisions every day – some are simple and routine, like deciding what to wear or choosing what to eat for lunch, while others are complex and life-altering, like what career path to take or which relationship is right for you. We're always facing new situations that require new decisions, and for many people this can bring up confusion, uncertainty, and anxiety. When you're not clear on what you want, you waste precious mental energy as you're stuck in deliberation. You might doubt yourself and your capabilities as the indecision leads to overthinking and inaction. Not knowing what you want can become an identity that causes you to feel unsure and doubtful about the future. I know this because I used to be the most indecisive person you could ever meet.

Around eight years ago, many of my anxieties were brought to the surface when I went for a routine eye test and was told that my prescription had changed and I needed a new pair of glasses. I walked onto the shop floor and looked out at the expanse of choice – row upon row of glasses – and I immediately felt overwhelmed. As I asked myself which pair I should choose, I went into panic mode. I walked around the store trying on pair after pair and, with every pair I tried on, I became more confused and overwhelmed. I started googling what the latest celebrities were wearing and looked to Ryan Gosling and David Beckham for inspiration, but I still couldn't decide. I asked the sales assistant working in the store to help me pick a pair and she looked with me. I had to be certain they would be the right pair. After trying some on, she gave me the nod on a pair, which I eventually settled on.

As I got out my card to pay, I felt doubt enter my mind. I'd just spent an hour in the store choosing a pair of glasses, but now I was questioning whether I'd made the right decision. After some internal wrangling, I paid and left. When I got to the London Underground station, I went down the escalator and, as I did so, I began to change my mind. The thoughts raced through my brain: *Maybe I don't need them. I'm here now so why don't I just go back and cancel the order.* I decided to go back up the escalator, but on the way up, I changed my mind and went back down again. I did this four times before I got to the bottom of the escalator and gave myself a stern talking to and finally went home. It was just a pair of glasses, yet in that moment, it felt like life and death.

Two years later and I was at Gatwick airport ready to fly to Las Vegas to play in the World Series of Poker. I needed a new pair of sunglasses as my last pair had broken and, after I'd checked in my luggage and gone through security, I looked up and spotted a sunglasses shop. A wave of dread pulsed through me and the thought popped into my head, *Not again*, but the dread soon passed because I knew that things were different now. I walked in, saw a pair of sunglasses I liked, picked them up, tried them on, paid for them, and walked out. I didn't once doubt my choice after I'd bought them, and I still wear them to this day.

What was different? Why did one decision feel like life or death and yet the other was fun, free, and easy? Would you take your time buying a pair of glasses or would it be easy for you? Have you ever been frozen when making a relatively simple choice? Choices are personal for each of us; some are easy and others are agonizing.

EXERCISE

Think about a time in the past when you couldn't decide. What made it tough for you? Why didn't you know what you wanted? Maybe this is a daily occurrence. Which day-to-day decisions are the most challenging? Where do you find decisions effortless and easy?

Decisions are what shape your life, and you have the power to make them. It's time to delve into your decision-making processes to see what makes them a challenge. We'll explore how you can start enjoying the process and have full access to making them. Feelings of uncertainty and doubt can be released, and the decisive version of you that knows what you want can be unleashed and, with it, you can create the life you really want.

Why Are Decisions So Hard?

Choice is amazing, it's freedom. We have the freedom to choose whatever we want, whenever we want, and yet so many of us give that freedom away as we'd prefer not to have to decide. So, why do we find it so hard to make decisions? Decisions follow three simple steps: The first is choice, where you see the options available to you. The second step is deliberation, where you evaluate the options and weigh up the pros and cons. This phase is where most people get stuck. The third and final step is commitment – this is where you decide which option you want and commit to it by taking action. It's important to know that a decision hasn't been made until you take action. Many people say they've 'decided' to set up a business or start a fitness routine, or leave a relationship that no longer serves them, but the decision hasn't been made until the intention is brought to life with action, a commitment that makes the idea a reality. It's easy to say it; it's another thing to do it.

The reason why decisions are hard is because you think you can get them wrong. 'Right' and 'wrong' are judgments, which we'll explore later in this chapter, and it's these judgments that create a great deal of unnecessary suffering. So, why do we fear getting decisions wrong? As a child, many of your decisions are made for you. If, over time, you weren't encouraged to think for yourself, make your own choices, and take accountability for those decisions, you can form the belief that someone else knows best or, if you wait long enough, someone else will decide for you. If you were criticized a lot for making choices that people didn't agree with or you were corrected often, you may have learned there's a 'right' or perfect way of doing things. This can cause you to spend your whole life looking for the right way to do things or agonizing over making the right choice and fearing making a wrong choice, leaving you afraid of making decisions.

Difficulty making decisions can result in you avoiding making decisions altogether, or passively waiting for things to improve and defaulting to accepting undesirable situations because you don't think you can change them. Over time, this way of thinking can become a costly habit, where decisions feel scary or impossible to make and no matter what choice you go for, you feel the outcome will be negative. This makes anything new a challenge to be avoided and starting new things an uncomfortable option.

> ### LENS CHECK
>
> Take a moment to reflect on what life is like for the world's most indecisive person, who questions every decision and agonizes over every tiny detail. What do decisions feel like for them? What does the future feel like for them? Unsure of what to do and when, how do they approach work and their relationships?

Many of us gave away our decision-making power earlier in life and never learned how much choice we really have. It's time to put the past in the past and wake up to the truth that decisions are your path to freedom and, in any moment – even right now – you have the opportunity to make a new decision that could alter the course of your life. Decisions can be exciting and fun; they can be something you look forward to. You can decide what you want, solve your problems, take ownership of your life, and claim your power with a decision. Don't give your decisions away; it's time to start making them.

Start with the Most Important Decision

The first place to start is with a decision. That's right, in order to step into your power and activate your decision-making abilities, you need to make the decision that you're a great decision-maker. This means committing to making decisions regularly. Imagine what a difference it would make to your life if you started choosing with power and conviction.

Each day you have many chances to make decisions – from planning your day and deciding what to eat or wear, to choosing what to work on and when. Practice being decisive about what you want and, if you find yourself in a situation where you don't know, make a quick choice anyway. If you're debating what to wear, set a timer for two minutes and choose. If you're out at lunch and the menu seems overwhelming, just pick one thing you like, even if you feel uncertain. See these mini choice points as a chance to practice being decisive. Give up sitting on the fence and saying, 'I don't mind' or 'I'm not sure.' Napoleon Hill, author of *Think and Grow Rich*, studied the most successful people in the world and found that those who failed made decisions slowly and changed them quickly, but those who succeeded made decisions quickly and changed them slowly.

Start making decisions and being a decisive person and shed the identity of someone who doesn't know what they want. Make decisions faster and more often and you'll get better at it. This first decision is the seed that will grow your decision-making muscle.

EXERCISE

An affirmation is a declaration that's used to reinforce a belief or desired outcome. It's making a conscious choice about the words you say to yourself. Affirmations direct your subconscious mind and, with repetition, they can create new automatic ways of thinking, creating new beliefs. A belief is a thought you keep thinking over time until it feels true for you.

For the next week, every time you catch yourself feeling indecisive, repeat the affirmation: 'I am decisive and I enjoy making decisions.' Say it to yourself three times and mean it as you say it. These mental reps will strengthen the belief you have in your decision-making capacity.

Being a decisive person also means giving up any past identity of going with the flow or fitting in with what others want. Being decisive means knowing what you want, and this means making it OK for you to want what you want. It's not selfish and it's not inconsiderate – it's your right, so exercise it. Some people feel it's selfish to want what they want, others feel they're not worthy, and some feel like they're not allowed to. Make a new decision today that it's OK for you to want what you want. Why do this? Because you have the right to make that decision – you choose your value, your thoughts, and what you want, and this starts with a decision inside you. You get to choose what you think, that's your freedom. Old decisions can be changed. Give yourself the permission. If you need someone else to give you it, then I'm formally giving you the nod right now.

Let Go of the Need for Certainty

I recently felt lost and unclear on what my next move should be with my coaching practice: Should I run events, focus on group coaching, do more speaking, or create an online course? So, I went out for a late evening stroll along the peaceful country roads near my house, which are surrounded by beautiful fields. When I feel lost, I know that space is a great place to find the answers. I walked, I got quiet, and I asked myself the question, 'What do I want?' Nothing was coming up, I was drawing a blank, so I kept walking and let my thinking settle even more and, a few moments later, the answer popped into my head: *You'll only know what you want when you let go of needing a guarantee that it will work out how you want it to.* I was reminded in that moment what I know well but often forget: that it's impossible to see the path when you want a guarantee on how it will all turn out – this is what blinds you from knowing what you want.

You don't have a crystal ball, you can't know how it will play out, you can only know what you want and what your next step is. Wanting a guarantee is called 'playing it safe,' which will give you more of what you already have, even if that isn't what you want. As you let go of the need for certainty, the path will become clear and you'll be able to make decisions.

Let go of needing certainty in the outcome.

Your energy comes from having the power to make decisions and it gets sucked away when you need to know how decisions will work out, because this brings your attention to what you can't control and the unknown. The more you focus on the unknown, the more confused you become, and this creates decision paralysis.

In the first verse of the *Tao Te Ching*, Lao Tzu says, 'The mystery is the doorway to all understanding.' What I think he is pointing us toward is that when we stop attempting to control uncertainty, predict the unknown, and explain the unexplained, we can accept the mystery. When you stop thinking, *How will it all work out?* or *What if it fails?* or *What if I get it wrong?* you can start making decisions in the moment that align with what you really want. The reason the mystery is a gateway to all understanding is because when you stop focusing on the unknown and what you can't control, you let go and are free to see the answers. While demanding certainty, you see only smoke, and when you let go of this demand, the smoke settles and you can see clearly again.

Stop Worrying About Making the Right Choice

As we've touched on, something that drives fear and prevents decision-making is seeing choices as 'right' or 'wrong.' This makes choices feel heavy because you think there's a 50 percent chance of getting it wrong. But decisions are more complex than a simple right or wrong – this is the all-or-nothing thinking we explored in the last chapter rearing its head again. Each time you make a decision, you're placing bets with your time, money, and energy based on incomplete information. In the early stages of my career as a poker player, I wanted to get decisions right every time – I hated making mistakes and being wrong. In poker, if someone bets the size of the pot and you have a decision to call, you don't have to be right every time. By doing some simple math you can see that their bet, plus the size of the pot and your call, means that, when you call, you only have to be right 33 percent of the time to break even. If you believe your hand has a 40 percent chance of winning, calling is a good play. If you think your hand only has a 25 percent of winning, it's better to fold. This means you can be wrong a large percentage of the time and still be a winner. The same is true with your decisions – you don't need to get them right every time.

We label outcomes we don't want as wrong, a failure, or bad and we label what we do want as right, a success, or good, but if you consider the big picture, good can lead to bad and bad can lead to good. You might win the lottery only to lose it all, or you might get fired from your job only for your dream job to come knocking at your door. The relationship that ends in heartbreak might be the very thing that wakes you up to your true value and worth. My darkest days as a poker player led me on a path of personal growth and discovery that resulted in me finding purpose and fulfillment as a coach.

Each choice you make leads to the next and the more decisions you make, the better you get at making them, but to do this you need to let go of the idea of there being a right choice and trust yourself to make your best choice. Facing a decision is like being presented with a number of doors to open and not knowing what's behind them. When you fear getting it wrong, you hesitate and spend all your time trying to figure out what's behind each door. You fear that if you open the wrong door, you'll be trapped in a room you can never leave. The truth is that each door you open presents you with a new set of doors, and you get to play again. You might not like what's behind a door, but once you make a decision, you can always make another one.

Every decision is a calculated risk. When you accept that risk, you get better at making the calculations. You can't avoid risk and uncertainty, so instead of worrying about making the right or wrong choice, aim to make your best choice given the information you have. As Steve Jobs said, 'You can't connect the dots looking forward; you can only connect them looking backward. So you have to trust that the dots will somehow connect in your future.' You can do your best and your best is all you can do.

Accept That Downsides Are Part of the Process

A major block to making decisions comes from expecting your decision to have no downsides. Starting before you're ready means being willing to make decisions before you feel ready, despite the discomfort. Don't expect to make a perfect decision. Each decision you make will have upsides and downsides. Taking a new fitness class will improve your health but might mean waking up early; investing in stocks may lead to financial gains, but you may also have the disappointment of short-term losses. Leaving a relationship that doesn't serve you, gaining freedom and growth, may also mean finding a new home and the hassle that comes with moving. Studying for a degree will give you skills and a qualification but will also take a great deal of time and cost a lot of money. If you decide to have children, you get to experience the joy of holding your baby in your arms for their first moments on Earth, you get to watch your kid's first steps, and create a connection with them that lasts a lifetime. You'll also have sleepless nights, deal with meltdowns over giving them the wrong color cup, and lose around 50 hours a week of your free time. If you decide to use social media, you get to connect with friends, watch funny reels that make you laugh, and have access to incredible motivating, inspiring, and life-changing reels from yours truly, The Perception Coach. However, using social media can also drain your time and energy, distract you from your work, and make you compare your life to others when you could be focusing on your own journey.

Every decision has upsides and downsides, and if you wait for decisions to only have upsides you'll live in analysis paralysis. Accepting the downsides and seeing them as part of the process is an important step toward becoming decisive and starting before you're ready. As soon as you accept it's OK for there to be downsides, you can stop waiting for the perfect choice and instead make quick decisions, commit to them, and get into action.

EXERCISE

On the bigger decisions, an effective way to process the options is to get them out of your head and onto paper by making a list of pros and cons. Your brain can get confused with everything swirling around in it, so having all the data laid out in front of you can be an extremely useful part of your toolkit. An important note before you dive into this exercise is to use it as a tool to gain clarity, not as a way to put off a decision or procrastinate. Any tool can be used for productivity or procrastination, it just depends how we use it.

Grab your journal and a pen. Take the specific decision you have to make and write it at the top of a blank page. Beneath it, divide the page into two columns. Label one side 'pros' and the other side 'cons.'

In the pros column, list all the advantages of the decision and in the cons column, list all the disadvantages. Look at the impact each pro and con would have. Keep going until you have written down as many as you can think of.

Next, weigh up all the pros and cons against each other. It's not necessarily the number of items you have in each list – it's the weight of them that counts. Assign a weight to each item ranging from one to five based on how much it matters to you (five being the most and one the least). Add up the totals on each side to see which means more to you. Consider if the pros and cons have a short-term benefit or long-term consequence.

Now, review and reflect on what has come up for you. You may want to go for a walk to give yourself time to

allow your mind to process the options and what you've learned - as we'll explore next, your subconscious is a powerful processor. This will also give you time to connect with your gut. Pros and cons will help you with the logic side and your gut will provide inner insights.

Finally, make a decision and remember that the pros and cons list is a guide and not a rule - trust you know best and that there's not a wrong choice to make, but simply a choice. Give yourself a time limit on it, so you can make a decision before you feel ready. When you've made your choice, choose to accept the downsides as part of the journey. This will allow you to drop any inner resistance and align you with the choice you made.

When making decisions, you can draw on frameworks, strategy, and information, but you should also learn to listen within, because when you turn inward you get answers from a deeper wisdom that is playing a far bigger game for us than we know...

Connect to Your Intuition

Your logical mind is great at solving problems, such as riddles, puzzles, or math conundrums, but it will keep you stuck when making bigger or more-complex decisions as it searches for the certainty it can't possibly get. With a math problem, you can be certain that one plus one equals two, but many of your decisions are far more complex and uncertain. Which partner should you pick? Which career should you choose?

What business should you start? For many years, I felt like an intuitive person trapped in a logical person's mind, which is why buying glasses, playing poker, and making decisions felt so tough. There's a dance between our head and heart, and learning to use both is a mastery level skill. Your decisions can come from a deeper place and, when you connect with this place, it can be the difference between spending two hours in the glasses shop and knowing what you want with certainty. When I learned to set my logical mind aside and look inside for the answers, I started making decisions faster, with more clarity and more authenticity.

That internal nudge that says 'Leave,' 'Stay,' or 'Go now' comes from a place of knowing that's far beyond our logical mind. To connect to it involves letting go. In the same way that when you're a proficient driver, you don't have to think about every micro decision – you just get in the car, let go, and drive – your subconscious mind is a superpower when you learn to let go and trust it.

As a rule of thumb, when something is known and can be solved, use logic to figure it out. When it's complex, unknown, and uncertain, trust your intuition.

When you don't have access to your instincts, you might know something is off, but trying to explain it rationally or make sense of it forces you into a spin. This is what can keep you in a relationship, career, or situation you don't want, as, despite what you 'know' internally, you feel unsure about what to do. What's really happening is you're waiting for your logical mind to justify your inner feelings and, given your brain is trying to seek certainty and confirm your established biases, expectations, and beliefs, it won't do that for you. It's your job to trust your intuition and make choices based on your instinct before your logical mind is ready, as it will never feel ready.

A new future requires new decisions, and this won't fit in with your past ways of thinking and acting. Trust means to let go. When you let go, answers will arise from a place that exists before thought. This is where an idea hits you in the shower or on a walk or when you've stopped thinking about it; it comes to you from inside.

You'll face many new situations and options that you can't plan for that will require you to trust your instincts. Perhaps you've been on a date and, within five seconds, known the person wasn't a match for you. Or maybe you felt like your job wasn't right for you so you quit, only for someone to offer you a more exciting role the next day. For many poker players I work with, their gut tells them something is off during a hand so they make a crazy fold that no one understands, only for them to be shown the best hand and for their instincts to have been correct. Your intuition sees miles down the line, farther than you could know.

Connecting to your intuition takes courage and a willingness to trust yourself and make what might appear to be mistakes in the short term, which are really life lessons. This involves slowing down the mind chatter about what you 'should' do or what is 'right' and listening for the answer from deep inside of you. Notice what you think you 'should' do and then remove the should. Maybe you think you should follow your friend's advice over your own or you should take a job rather than set up your business. These 'shoulds' come from the expectations we explored in Chapter 1. As you look at your options free from this pressure, it will become clearer – it's amazing how much this simple action changes your level of clarity. The smoke clears and you can see the answer.

The key to hearing your intuition is to ask yourself questions and then get quiet and listen to what comes up.

EXERCISE

To access your inner knowing, take some time to relax and follow these three simple steps. First, get to a quiet place in your mind. Second, ask yourself the question you want an answer to. And third, get quiet again and let the answer come to you. You can affirm the word 'relax' to yourself as you settle down the chatter in your mind. Take some deep breaths to anchor yourself into the present, allowing any thoughts in your mind to settle, and when you feel at peace, ask yourself the following questions:

- **What do I really want?**
- **What do I think is the best option?**
- **How does this feel for me?**
- **If it was OK for me to fail, what would I do?**

Listening to and trusting your intuition is a practice – in the beginning, you might think you hear your intuition when really it's fear telling you what to do. Keep learning from what happens, take the lessons, and keep trusting. Trust your instincts. After all, trust is belief without proof – this is why it takes trust to listen to your instincts and to act on them. You don't know what's behind the door; you just have to trust which door feels right to you. You don't have the evidence yet, because you need to take the step to get the proof. Therefore, building a connection with your intuition requires you to take a leap of faith.

Don't expect to get it right all the time. You might date someone because you feel drawn to them and they turn out to be a bad choice. Keep trusting. You might set up a business only to have it fail. Keep trusting. You might study a university course only for it not to be the direction you wanted to go in. Keep trusting. People typically give up on their intuition when they don't get the outcome they wanted, or they beat themselves up for getting it wrong. You're allowed to make mistakes, but remember, don't view them as a wrong choice; instead, see them as lessons you're being guided to learn. If you stay open to learning from them, you'll expand your awareness and strengthen your connection with your intuition. You'll also become less fearful of getting it 'wrong.'

Ask yourself the following question to always stay in a place of trust, self-love, and growth: 'Why is this happening for me?' When you listen to yourself, you're trusting your inner wisdom to guide you and, when you act on it, you get feedback and you learn from the feedback, always. If you only rely on logic to make decisions, you'll end up in circles, repeating old patterns, trying to find certainty, when you and I both now know that certainty doesn't exist. It takes courage and faith to let go and listen to your intuition. You are part of the universe, and the wisdom of the universe is guiding you; it's time to trust it.

EXERCISE

One of the simplest yet most powerful ways to tap into your intuition when making a decision is to flip a coin. If you have two options and you're not sure which one to go with, the coin won't answer this dilemma for you; instead, it will show you your own answer. It will connect you to your inner guidance because the outcome of the coin will give you one of two feelings: confirmation or resistance. Say you're considering whether to quit your job or stay, so you flip a coin with heads being stay and tails being quit. If you flip the coin and it comes up heads and you feel disappointment, it tells you that staying isn't what you truly want. If it comes up heads and you feel relief or joy, then it's pointing you toward what you want.

Many people think you should blindly follow the coin's answer - you can do that if you want, but know that the coin reveals the answer that already lies inside of you.

Make a Commitment

The ultimate tool to becoming the most decisive person you know is to practice by getting committed. Being indecisive is living with a lack of commitment. As I mentioned at the start of this chapter, the third and final step of decision-making is commitment – a decision hasn't been made until you take action and commit to it.

People often hesitate when committing to something new, which is why the clients I work with often experience a personal breakthrough when they sign up to work with me, because signing up itself is a big commitment. I know what that feels like – it took me over six months of debating and agonizing in my mind before I made a big investment and hired my first coach. The moment I signed up, I felt a huge sense of relief and wished I'd done it sooner. When you sit there and spend hours thinking about what to do, you simply haven't committed yet and can't move forward. You're keeping your options open, waiting for something or someone better to come along. The moment you commit to a decision, you eliminate the other options – and this is often what terrifies people. This is why many people fear committing to a relationship, a new job, or a hobby. What if they want to do something else instead?

Consider where in your life you're keeping your options open. This is the breeding ground for FOMO, the fear of missing out. What's the cost of being indecisive and sitting on the fence? You experience doubt, fear, and uncertainty for longer. You can't get into action or enjoy the thing you want to do because you haven't made the choice, and so you live in a state of waiting.

As we've seen, consideration is an important element of making decisions as you assess your options, but it isn't a place to live in constantly. Living in a state of analysis paralysis has you overthinking, second-guessing, and, ultimately, fearing decision-making. The Latin word for decision is *decisio* and its root is *decidere*, which means 'to cut off.' When you make a decision, you commit by cutting off the other options. The moment before you decide, all your options are open, but you're in a state of waiting and therefore can't take action to move forward. It's a little like sitting in the car and having five destinations in your mind and not choosing any of them – you don't then go anywhere. The moment you choose your destination, you eliminate the other options and can begin your journey with purpose and excitement – you get to make progress. It's the moment before you decide when anxiety and doubt are at their highest.

Once you've made a decision, you have certainty about the direction you're moving in and you can get into action. This can look like joining the club, signing up for the course, leaving the job, setting up the business, enjoying the relationship, starting the podcast, or giving the presentation.

One of the most powerful ways to commit is with accountability. This is where you find someone who will hold you accountable to your decision or goal. This way, when doubt rises, you have someone on your team to help get you over the line. Some of the best ways to do this are to hire a coach or mentor, make a bet with a friend, share it publicly, or sign up and do something for charity. It will get you off the fence and into action. We all experience doubt and indecision, and external support can help you when this arises. Creating accountability is a great way to turn your idea into a committed decision.

The moment you commit to a decision fully you experience JOMO, the joy of missing out. You step out of no-man's land

and confusion and into the present moment. When you intentionally commit to a decision, you experience the inner peace, enjoyment, and satisfaction of no longer trying to be somewhere you're not and the fear that comes with that. There's no freedom in keeping your options open because you're neither here nor there and you don't get very far.

As we saw in the last chapter, most people wait until the discomfort and fear is gone before they commit – they want to feel ready; but the truth is feeling ready comes *after* you have committed. You don't have certainty about how it will all turn out, but you can be certain about what you choose to commit to, and this creates a new level of energy, excitement, and clarity.

Stop putting things off and start making decisions and committing to them. The more you practice committing, the better you'll get at making decisions by following through.

LENS CHECK

Take a moment to reflect on what life's like for the most decisive person in the world, who makes decisions with ease. They are sure about themselves and have clarity around what they do. How do they feel about making decisions? How do they feel about the future? They enjoy taking charge of choices and are a master at making the best choice in the moment. What's their approach to their career and relationships?

When you're connected with your inner wisdom and what you really want – not the logical what you 'should' want – you'll feel more connected with yourself. You can take charge of your life, set your direction, and uncover your why. It's time to dive more deeply into this with the next chapter.

KEY TAKEAWAYS

- **Make the conscious choice to be decisive and grab every opportunity you can to make decisions and take charge of your life.**
- **Let go of the idea that you can make a right or wrong choice; instead let your intuition tell you what's best for you. Each decision you make will present you with an outcome from which you can make new decisions.**
- **Notice when you feel resistance to committing to a decision and remind yourself that JOMO is waiting for you once you've made it.**

CHAPTER 3

Know What You Want

You picked up this book because something inside of you said you want to make a change. Maybe you want to grow personally or professionally, or reach your full potential. Perhaps you want to change your career or relationship, or maybe there's something you want to do but you don't know what that is yet. Many of the clients I work with aren't starting something because they just don't know what they want. And when you don't know what you want, you can end up drifting.

Imagine a ship on the ocean with no captain or crew. It's drifting along, driven by external forces – the wind, the waves, and the environment determine where it goes and, as a result, it may end up anywhere. This is what life feels like when you don't have purpose, direction, and goals to aim for. You may be doing a lot, you may even be productive and working hard, but you don't seem to get where you want to be, and it can feel like something is missing. If you don't know what you want, you might start and be in action just for the sake of it, rather than working toward something meaningful for you, or something that would genuinely improve your life.

Now imagine another ship on the ocean, but this time it has a captain and a crew onboard and a target destination. The ship may face the wind and waves, but the conditions don't determine its direction, the captain does. You are the captain. When you know where you're heading and why, your life takes on a whole new meaning and can become an exciting adventure. Your goals create a filter for your decisions and actions. When your goals are aligned with your purpose and values, starting can be something you're motivated to do, your decisions become easier, and your fears become simply part of the game. As Jim Rohn says, 'If the why is powerful, the how is easy.'

In this chapter, we'll explore the steps to uncovering your goals, values, and purpose so you can take the next step toward your dreams, whatever they are for you. But first, let's look at what stops us from knowing where we're going and why.

How Fear Gets in the Way

Fear is such a common block when it comes to getting started that I've dedicated a whole chapter to it (*see Chapter 7*). For now, though, let's look at how it stops us from knowing what we really want and setting goals.

In my experience, there are two fears at play here. Firstly, there's the fear of failure, which we touched on in Chapter 1. What if you set the goal and you don't make it or get it wrong – won't that be embarrassing, disappointing, and mean you're not good enough? When you think about a goal, your fears around it will come up and, often, those fears are so big that they can stop you from dreaming at all. Many times I'll ask people what they want and they can't give me an answer – this is very normal, so if this is you, rest assured that you're not alone and we'll address this so you can discover what you want.

Linked to the fear of failure is the second fear – the fear of success. This is a fear of not being worthy of the goal. Maybe you think, *Who am I to go for that?* Or perhaps you think, *I don't deserve that kind of success.* Here's the truth: The fear of success is simply the fear of failure in disguise, because if you really were to succeed and achieve what you want, then the possibility of failure would feel even more daunting. There would be more to lose and more that you could fail at, and that really would mean you're not good enough and everyone would find out (this is impostor syndrome at play, and we'll look closely at how to overcome this in Chapter 5). It's one thing failing in the minor leagues, but when you reach the heights of success, you have farther to fall.

Let's consider the fear of success and failure as two sides of the same coin and their job is to keep you in your comfort zone. We like to act in accordance with our current self-image and we don't stray too far away from it. If your success level is 50 percent and you go to 60 percent success, fear starts to kick in and you retreat. This is why people who gain money often give it away and people who lose weight often put it back on. Your outer goals are a reflection of your inner identity, and your brain works hard to keep this consistent.

LENS CHECK

Take a moment to reflect on what life's like for someone who has no purpose and direction. They haven't got any goals and lack motivation and energy. What does their day-to-day look like? Where are they headed? How difficult are their decisions? How do they feel about themselves? How does their self-image keep them stuck? How do they feel about life?

New results require a new you. The person who achieves your goal is a different person to the you who is here now. So three things need to happen. First, you need to be willing to let go of your current identity. Second, you need to be willing to step into a new identity and, third, you need to give yourself permission to feel worthy of being this person and achieving this success. This means refusing to buy into the fears, excuses, and beliefs that want to keep you at your current success percentage. If you're at 50 percent success, now is the time to see yourself at 90 or 100 percent. When your self-image changes on the inside, your world shifts on the outside to match. With this awareness, you can make the decision that it's OK for you to go after what you want.

EXERCISE

Think about a goal you'd like to achieve – it could be a dream relationship, career, amount of wealth, health, or traveling the world. Pick something that feels exciting for you, write it down in a journal, and feel what it would be like to have it. As you do, notice what negative thoughts

come up, such as 'I don't deserve it,' 'It's too out of reach,' or 'People like me don't do that.' Whatever comes up is what's stopping you from either setting goals or getting started on them. This inner resistance is like a rope tied to you that stops you from stepping out of your comfort zone and getting what you want.

To cut the rope, take each negative thought and turn it into a positive one that supports your goal. For example, 'I deserve this,' or 'Achieving this goal will give me valuable skills,' or 'I'll become the person I've always wanted to be.' When you find those negative thoughts hiding in the fear of failure, you can eliminate them, and you'll be surprised at how fast your dreams become reality.

Identify What You Want

One Sunday evening in August 2016, as I sat in my flat in Clapham, London, I decided I wanted a different future. I was frustrated with my life. I'd been chasing after success and watched it run away from me time and time again. As I mentioned in the Introduction, I'd read and listened to many personal development resources without acting on what I was learning. I passively consumed information waiting to feel ready, but, at this point in my life, I'd had enough; it was time for a change.

I wrote out how I wanted my life to be in seven different areas: personal growth, relationships, health, career, fun and hobbies, finances, and contribution. I wrote down in the present tense what I wanted in specific detail. I was single at the time and hadn't had any joy in the romance area of my life. I allowed myself to dream. For relationships, I wrote, 'I am feeling happy and content as I stare into the eyes of my wife. I'm so happy to have found someone beautiful who I care for and who equally cares for me. We want to help each other grow and build a life together. I have two wonderful children who I help support and fulfill their dreams.' Although I didn't know it at the time, with that decision, I had just set the wheels in motion on my dream future. I read this vision statement each day for six months, visualized it being true, and then I let it go, as if it was already done.

Happiness will arrive the moment you take a step toward it.

On March 4, 2017, the lady I wanted to meet walked into my life. A year later, we were engaged. That September, we got married, a year later we had our daughter, and then, two years later, our son. Up until this point, I simply didn't know what I wanted. I had never taken the time to write it down or dare myself to dream and, as a result, I got what life gave me. By writing out my goals, I took the very first step to making them real. Being clear on what I wanted helped me to filter out what I didn't want. I trusted my intuition, listened to it, and acted in alignment with my goals, not my fears. Now, every year, I look at my goals list or vision board and smile when I see the goals as already completed. One thing I can tell you with certainty is that what you really want is possible for you, you are worthy of it, and you don't have to wait until you achieve it to be happy.

What do you really want?

When you know your goals, your choices in life get easier. Your goals act as a filter for what you say 'yes' or 'no' to. The most important question you can ask yourself is, 'What do I really want?' It's easy to spend your life thinking what you *should* want or what would make others happy, but it's time to start thinking about what *you* really want, so you can live a life aligned with your highest self. From this place, you'll have more to give to others than you ever could have imagined, and you'll know what to start taking action on. You might not feel ready, but you'll know what direction you're heading in, and all you have to do is take the first tiny step.

Allow yourself to dream. If you find that some resistance comes up, lean into it – that's what starting before you're ready is all about. If I'd stayed in my comfort zone, I never would've thought I could get married and start a family. If you have resistance, which is perfectly normal when deciding what you want, notice it, get comfortable with the discomfort, and affirm to yourself that it's OK to go after what you want. Close your eyes, allow yourself to time travel 12 months into the future, and see that you have achieved everything you wanted and you're the person you want to be. What do you see? What does it feel like? What are you doing? What results have you created? There really are no limits to what you can decide to create – the future version of you is waiting to be birthed. Now, allow all the possible answers to come from this future place. This is your permission slip to explore what you really want, free from limitations and fears. Once you've connected with what you want, it's time to complete the exercise below.

EXERCISE

For each of the following areas, write down what you'd really want if anything was possible for you. If you're reading this book because you want to get started in one specific area, then choose that. If you're unsure about what you want or where to start, that's OK – just write out your answers to all the areas and you'll find that clarity will come. If you still don't know, write down a list of everything you *don't* want – either results in your life now or in the future.

Then, next to each result, flip it to what you do want. For example, if you wrote, 'I don't want to be in debt,' flip it to 'I want to be financially free.' Or if you wrote, 'I don't want to be single,' write alongside it, 'I want a partner who appreciates me for who I am.' In the words of Tony Robbins, 'Put the book down and write this out now.' Not when you feel ready, but now. You'll thank me later.

Write down what you want in the following areas:

1. **Personal growth**
2. **Relationships**
3. **Health**
4. **Career**
5. **Fun and hobbies**
6. **Finances**
7. **Contribution**

Write out your answers in the present tense, for example, 'I am working three days a week,' 'I am in a loving relationship,' or 'I weigh 70 kilograms and I love my body.'

Write down how you want things to be as if they are already true. Don't get bogged down in the details yet – their time will come. You only need your end goal and your first steps, and the rest will be revealed as you go along.

Next, write down steps you can take in that area to move you toward it. If your goal is to lose 4 kilograms, your steps may be to meal plan, eat healthily, and cut out alcohol. Think about how this shapes your decisions, thoughts, and habits. When your friend asks if you want a glass of wine, you already know your response because your goal is set.

Once you've done this, take the three goals you feel would have the biggest impact on your life and circle them. Next to each answer, write down *why* you want it. If you wrote, 'I am working three days a week,' now write why this is important to you. Maybe it gives you more time with your children or to play golf or go to the gym. Maybe it's the freedom you've always dreamed of having. The goal is the destination and the why is the fuel that gets you there.

Then write down what it would cost you to *not* achieve this goal. This can be a powerful motivator due to loss aversion, a concept in behavioral economics discovered by Daniel Kahneman and Amos Tversky. We're often motivated more by what we'll lose versus what we'll gain. For example, the pain of losing $100 is greater than the pleasure of gaining $100. You can use this principle to your advantage, using the fear as fuel for your goals.

Finally, write out the steps you can take to make each of your three most important goals a reality.

Harness the Power of Visualization

The goals you identified in the exercise above will now become the three goals you'll visualize each day. There are a few key reasons why this is worth doing.

Writing them down is the first step to turning your goals into a physical reality. Reminding yourself of your goals daily by visualizing them is essential for staying on the path and not getting distracted.

The next reason to visualize your goals each day is to make the unfamiliar familiar. Your future goal is not yet manifest. It's simply an idea, and it may feel uncomfortable and trigger the fears we looked at earlier in this chapter. A new goal will require a new version of you to achieve it. By visualizing yourself as the version of you that has completed it, feeling what that feels like, and imagining what you'd be doing if you'd achieved it, you merge that new you with your present self.

As you immerse yourself in the visualization, you mentally experience the success, abundance, or health you desire. The brain doesn't know the difference between what's real and what's imagined, so, as you imagine yourself as the person you want to be and feel worthy of achieving what you want, you'll start to change your self-image and what your subconscious believes is possible for you.

This is why manifesting and visualizing have become so popular in recent years – they've always worked and now there's science that backs them up.

EXERCISE

To visualize your goals, close your eyes and take a deep breath. Hold your breath for five seconds and exhale slowly and completely. Repeat this three times and allow yourself to relax fully.

As your breathing returns to a steady state, imagine yourself already having achieved your goal. See yourself doing what you would be doing and feeling what you would be feeling, and look through the eyes of this version of yourself. What do you see, hear, and feel? Notice how you feel having already acquired what you want. Connect emotionally and feel the peace, joy, confidence, or relaxation it brings.

Finally, feel gratitude for achieving your goal and enjoying the benefits of it, and then let it go. Take a few more deep breaths, then open your eyes and go about the rest of your day, relaxed in the knowledge that your goal is on its way.

As you let go of the visualization and go about your day, your subconscious will be scanning for opportunities and aligning you with them. Maybe you want to start a new job, create more wealth, meet your dream partner, or improve your health. By placing the version of yourself that has already achieved it in your head, you're informing your brain of what's important to you.

The reticular activating system (RAS) is a network of neurons in the brain stem that filters information based on what your brain deems important. Visualization programs the RAS to scan for people, information, ideas, and situations that are relevant to your goal. It does this by itself – all you need to do is sit down for a few minutes each day and show it what to scan for and then let go and trust it to work on your behalf, like your own personal assistant. When you focus on your goal each day in a relaxed way, your brain will do the work for you to help you attract what you want.

Use Your Values as a Compass

Your values are the underlying principles, beliefs, and standards that guide your actions, decisions, and priorities. They represent what matters to you most in life – like honesty, trust, loyalty, family, freedom, or growth – and they're your compass. There are no right values – they aren't good or bad and they're not universal; they're what is true and important for *you*.

One of my favorite coaching questions to ask is, 'What are you making important here?' It gets people present to whether they're being driven by fear, by what they think they *should* do, or by what they value. Your values guide your decisions, helping you make choices that align with who you are. If you currently value certainty, comfort, and convenience, then starting won't be an appealing option for you, because, as we've seen, you need to step into the unknown, get uncomfortable, and take calculated risks while you learn a new skill, discipline, or action. Those values might not align with what you really want.

When I set up my page on social media and posted every day, I risked judgment, and it took an immense amount of effort, consistency, and planning. I did it because I valued growth, authenticity, and making a difference to others. If I didn't, I would've quickly given up. This made it a must for me, even on the days when I didn't feel like posting. In Chapter 1, we explored the musts and expectations that are placed on you by others, that you often take on unconsciously. Chosen values are musts that *you* want – they're the standards you choose for yourself.

When I ask people in workshops how they got through the most challenging times in their lives, they almost always give the same answer, 'I had to.' This is because their values were so strong they didn't see any other options available to them and their decision was made. Values give personal meaning to your actions and, when you're grounded in the values that are most aligned and connected to who you are, even some of the most challenging situations can become ones you lean into. You'll feel 'off' when your values are not being upheld, and you'll feel aligned when they are.

If you value health yet you eat junk food and don't exercise, it will hurt you mentally and emotionally. If you value honesty and your boss asks you to lie to a team member, this will cause a conflict within you. Conflicting values make decisions a challenge, which is why knowing your values and aligning with them is essential to making powerful decisions and finding meaning in the projects you want to start. When your values are aligned with your actions, you won't need to feel ready to act.

Typically, your core values stay the same – they're a part of who you are – but your values can change as you grow and as your goals shift. In my 20s, I valued going out partying and drinking. I now value staying in with a good book and a cup of tea. Your values are personal to you, where you're at in life, and what's important to you. Don't compare yourself to others; focus on what matters most to you.

EXERCISE

Think of a time when you felt most proud, fulfilled, or happy. What was happening? Why did it feel meaningful? What values were present? Write it down and connect with what was going on and what it meant to you. What were the driving values behind this? What did it take? Was it courage, humility, trust, friendship, love, honesty, growth, connection, or passion?

Next, think about a time in the past when you felt most angry, frustrated, or hurt. What was happening? Why did it feel so painful? This can reveal when your deeply held values were broken, conflicted, or violated. You may not have known it at the time, but looking back now, what values do you feel were being compromised? Maybe someone broke your trust, let you down, or wasn't reliable. Anger is often a healthy sign that your values are being challenged or you're frustrated about something.

Now, think about someone you admire – perhaps a role model, a valued friend, or a mentor. What traits do you respect in them? This can point you toward values you'd like to have. Is there a teacher who was firm but fair and

so displayed integrity, or perhaps a movie star who is kind and gives back from a place of service, or a parent who was always honest with you?

Take all the values you've written down from these three reflections and put them aside for a moment while we look at where you're at now. What values are guiding your current decisions? Which of these do you want to keep and which no longer serve you? If you value certainty, then you may want to value courage instead. If you value comfort, look at how it conflicts with your goals. Which values would you need to be a powerful force in achieving your goals? Now, list your values in order of importance and select the five that you feel most deeply connected to. You can use these to help guide your goals, decisions, and actions. In choosing these values you'll have a compass to direct you as you step into the unknown and start before you're ready.

What Do You Need?

Closely related to values are needs. While values are about who you are and what you believe, needs are an essential requirement for your physical, emotional, and mental well-being. Your core needs are food, emotional safety, self-worth, alone time, exercise, and a roof over your head. When your fundamental needs are not met, your decisions and goals will revolve around meeting them, and this can cause a great deal of inaction.

While values are more stable, your needs address your comfort, survival, and safety in the moment, based on where you are, who you're with, and the circumstances you're in. For example, someone who is at a BBQ and is hungry needs food, and so their primal goal and decisions will revolve around what to eat and when. If they've eaten earlier, their needs may be more focused on connecting with others, playing games, and enjoying themselves.

When your needs are met, it will take you out of survival mode and into a place of inner safety where you can be true to yourself and not have to compromise your values, authenticity, and goals. This is vitally important to having the ability to start. When you're starting something new from a place of lack, insecurity, and neediness, it makes it hard to step into the unknown. It's like building a house on quicksand. You focus on trying to make yourself feel safe, instead of playing to win. It not only distracts you from your goals, it causes you to freeze.

Unmet needs can conflict with your values. If your needs aren't met, you may find yourself compromising your values to meet them. For example, seeking approval from others because you don't approve of yourself, working a job you hate because you need the money, or pretending to like someone you don't.

The secret is to meet your own needs. Unmet needs become unconscious goals driving your behavior, but when your needs are met you're free to choose what you really want. Gaining approval becomes optional, the relationship becomes optional, the new hobby or project becomes an exciting prospect to take on.

EXERCISE

Write down all the things you need: These aren't 'nice to haves,' they're what make you feel safe, secure, and happy. Some examples are financial security, love, friendship, self-worth, mental health, well-being, acceptance, peace, or alone time. Which of your needs are not currently being met? How do you meet your core needs currently? What would be some ways you can meet these needs that align with your values?

Make a commitment to meet your core needs yourself. If you need love, love yourself from within, be kind to yourself, and appreciate yourself. If you need finances, search for a job or an additional income stream. Although you can seek support from those around you, meeting your own needs will give you a deeper sense of security and, from this place, you'll be free to start, take risks, and take inspired action. Starting will become something exciting instead of a threat to your survival.

Use Purpose as Your Power

There's a grand purpose we're all here for and this will be revealed to you as you meet your needs, live from your values, and get started on your goals. Along the way, you'll start to see that patterns show up – opportunities present themselves and a calling to something greater than yourself is revealed.

Purpose is available to you in every moment of every day. It comes down to why you're doing what you do. I remember the first time this clicked for me. It was Christmas and my mum wanted to walk to visit my grandad, who we call Pop. It was a 10-minute drive or a 45-minute walk and the weather was miserable. My mum, my dad, and I set off on the walk. Within five minutes, I was huffing and puffing, and I found myself thinking, *Why didn't we just take the car?* But we hadn't taken the car, we were walking. As my frustration continued to build and the pressure kept rising in my head, it suddenly dawned on me: I could spend the next 45 minutes complaining and frustrated or I could simply enjoy it, so I decided to give the walk a purpose.

I made the decision that I would make the next 45 minutes about my mum. I would ask her questions and be genuinely interested in her answers. I would make this a fun walk for her. I started asking her questions and the time flew by. She showed me the flowers in people's gardens and explained the names and origin of them. I felt connected to my mum and enjoyed the stroll and, by the time we got to Pop's house, I was in a great mood and gave him the same level of attention and curiosity I'd given to my mum. I remember that day well, and now, years later, Pop is no longer with us, and I look back fondly on that day and the times I went to see him in his later years, applying the same purpose to each visit – to find out about him.

On one visit, I remember him telling me that he was 90 and could no longer dance. He said he missed it and desperately wished he could dance again. He said to me, 'You're still young, you can dance and travel and live, so do it now while you can.' He inspired me to live with more passion, to do what I love, and stop waiting! It set me in motion to take bold actions, focus on what matters, and to give this life everything I have now.

You can find purpose in everything you do by asking yourself, 'What does it mean to me?' and 'What do I want it to mean?' You can start anything, anytime you want, because it's important to you. You just need to know why you're doing it. When you make whatever you're starting about someone or something you care about, the 'how' becomes a formality. You don't complain about the task, how tough it is, or how much effort it will take, you simply remind yourself why you're doing it or who you're doing it for. When you're doing it for the sake of it, or to please someone else, or going to a job you don't care about just to pay the bills and get by, then it will feel pointless and like hard work. You're like the ship with no crew – you may reach destinations sometimes, but there's no passion behind it. This is the default life. When you focus on what it means to you, on serving others, and the difference you can make by taking actionable steps, it becomes easy to write the book that changes someone's life, start the podcast that brings joy to others, cook the meal for your partner that makes them feel appreciated, go to the job to build a better future for your family, or set up the project that benefits the community. You do things because they matter to you.

So, ask yourself:

- 'What do I want to start doing?'
- 'Why is it important to me?'
- 'What does it mean to me?'
- 'What do I want it to mean to me?'

- 'Why am I doing it?'
- 'Who am I doing it for?'
- 'What difference can it make to the lives of others?'
- 'How does this link to my values?'
- 'Who will I become as a result of achieving this?'

Define What Success Means for You

The moment you set a goal, know your values, and are on a path you have chosen, you're a success. This is why chasing success to impress others or gain money for the sake of it and only for the reward itself is a trap. Each of us has our own unique gifts and each of us has our own path. For me, I'm obsessed with what drives us, what gives life meaning, and how you can fulfill your potential, so I enjoy deep conversations, writing, coaching, and speaking. To someone else that would be boring. Money is an important factor for many people and having it is very useful, but if it's the *only* factor or measure of success, it can cause you to spend your whole life chasing the goal only to get there and think, *What was the point?* Money has no meaning in itself; it's what you do with it that matters. A job can be a gateway to a hobby, a passion, or something you love to do.

What's your default definition of success? Maybe it's having a certain amount of money, fame, or recognition. Be honest with yourself and write it down. Does this definition of success feel authentic to you? Does it make you feel alive? Does it come from you or from society? Does it align with your values? If the answer is 'yes,' then great. If it's a 'no,' maybe there's something more you want and, if so, ask yourself this question: 'What do I want success to mean to me?' If you're living from your own definition of success, then you're already successful – you don't have to wait until you've 'made it.'

> *'It is better to follow your own path, however imperfectly, than to follow someone else's perfectly.'*
>
> The Bhagavad Gita

Most people work a job, seek a partner, or pursue a goal to become successful. Then they reach the goal and think, *Is this it?* You can be successful now by doing something you love, something that excites you, or something you're passionate about. Motivational speaker and author Earl Nightingale once said, 'Success is the progressive realization of a worthy goal or ideal.' For some this is teaching, for others it's painting or playing poker, for some it's working alone and for others it's being part of a team. We all have our own version of success. What's yours?

LENS CHECK

Take a moment to reflect on what life's like for someone who is clear on their values, meets their own needs, and knows their purpose and direction. They have clear goals they're excited about and plan their course with certainty and excitement. What meaning does their life have? What does the future feel like for them? How do they pursue their goals? They see opportunities everywhere and easily filter decisions through their goals and purpose. They live in alignment with their core values. How easy are their choices? How do they feel about themselves and their life?

As you move forward in alignment with your values and bring meaning to what you do, the path will unfold. You'll start and keep on starting, as every goal accomplished is the start of a new one. You'll have a reason behind why you do what you do, giving you choice, meaning, and motivation, even when it gets tough. The journey never ends. You're always starting – don't wait to feel ready.

Even when you're clear on where you're going and why, an obstacle that can distract you from this vision is overthinking. Next, we're going to explore how to master your mind so you can get out of your head and into action.

KEY TAKEAWAYS

- **Know your goals and align your identity with what you want. Stay focused and visualize your goals each day to keep them front of mind and allow your brain to support you in achieving them.**
- **Get clear on your values and meet your own needs. Your values serve as your compass to keep you on the path, and you'll be operating from a secure space when your needs are met first by you.**
- **Remember that you can find meaning in any situation. By uncovering your why, you give your goals purpose and have the motivation to take action in the face of challenges.**

CHAPTER 4

Escape the Overthinking Trap

When starting anything new, it's natural to think about what you have to do, what might go wrong, and all the possible options. But overthinking happens when you get stuck in the habit of worry, rumination, indecision, and analysis paralysis, and you spend too long in your head and not enough time in action. You might catch yourself replaying past events over and over again and wishing they were different. Thinking is helpful, but too much of it hurts.

Rumination is when you repeatedly focus on thoughts, emotions, and experiences without reaching a solution or closure. This is a passive process in your mind and can happen for minutes, hours, days, weeks, months, or even years if you obsess over the same problems and don't resolve them. You might circle around on a decision or situation, playing out all the possible scenarios and outcomes. *Should I do this, or should I do that?* The 'what ifs' run wild in your mind as you think about what might happen or what could go wrong. It can lead to trouble sleeping, as your mind races and you can't stop thinking about a situation, and the more you try to make the thoughts stop, the more they continue to frustrate you.

All this overthinking can also lead you to distractions. Not only do the thoughts take you away from what you want to do, but the discomfort of having to experience the doubt, worry, and negative ruminations can drive you to seek a distraction, where you turn to your phone, scroll social media, or binge-watch TV to avoid dealing with the never-ending mental chatter. These distractions further interrupt you from resolving the issues, keeping your problems alive and you stuck.

In this chapter, we'll look at strategies to help you break free of overthinking so you can stop waiting to feel ready. Before we get stuck in, though, let's explore why we get stuck in rumination in the first place.

What Are You Holding on to?

Overthinking is caused by both internal fears and uncertainty. Our thoughts and feelings create a need for control as the mind tries to predict, analyze, or solve any perceived threats to our security, identity, or well-being. There's thinking and then there's too much thinking. When it comes to overthinking, you're holding on to a thought, situation (past or present), or person and can't let go. You're trying to escape reality in your thoughts, ruminating about something instead of being in action.

The ego is the part of the mind that creates our sense of self; it's what makes each of us separate beings. Its role is to seek control and certainty, and it strives to protect your sense of identity at all costs. In an attempt to keep you safe, your ego drives overthinking by creating an emotional dependency on outcomes, people, or situations to try to gain control. The ego relies on comparison, judgment, and attachment to maintain its narrative of who you are. This leads to a constant need to analyze, control, or secure what you're afraid of losing. This dependency generates the fear of loss, uncertainty, or failure, which fuels the mind to overanalyze every detail, replay past events, or worry about the future in an attempt to protect what feels vital to your well-being. It's the mind's way of clinging to attachments and using thinking as a survival strategy to try to prevent perceived threats from happening. It can feel like to stop thinking would be to kill the ego, which is why at times it can feel so hard to let go of thoughts because, to your ego, this can feel unsafe.

When you attach to an outcome, person, or thought, it keeps you stuck there, leading to anxiety, stress, frustration, or doubt. Detachment is the flip side, where you withdraw from people or situations, mentally or emotionally. Signs you're detached include feeling indifferent or disconnected, or feeling a lack of motivation or zest for life. Attachment can feel like watching your team in the World Cup final and detachment is like watching a football match with no care who wins. With attachment you're all in and with detachment you're all out.

The key to breaking free from overthinking is non-attachment. This is a state of being connected and engaged with what you're doing without holding on. You care, but you know you can let go if you want to. With attachment, you're holding on without the awareness that you can let go, and with detachment, you have fully let go and aren't involved. Non-attachment allows you to hold a thought, emotion, goal, relationship, or project and experience it fully, without identifying with it and without it controlling you. You feel all the emotions, hear the thoughts, and experience them, without losing your 'self' to them.

Once, I was on my way to deliver a personal development workshop for a company in central London when the train stopped. I had left in plenty of time, but the train had been stuck for half an hour, and it was becoming apparent I was going to be late. My mind started to race. I got off the train at Westminster to get a taxi and, as I did, I saw gridlock traffic for miles around me. The thoughts raced even more. I hailed a taxi and got in, knowing I'd be late. My mind kept jumping around: *What would people think? Would people be mad? Would this ruin my career? This is unprofessional. I have to get there on time.* I felt the panic and anxiety rising in me and my thoughts continued to race.

I messaged the company that had hired me to let them know I'd be late. I wanted to get there on time, but there wasn't much more I could do. My mind was trying to find something to control, anything, but in that moment, I realized I wasn't in control. I let go of my attachment to being on time – this was driving my racing mind; I was holding on. I figured that I could show up exhausted and anxious from all the overthinking, which wouldn't serve the participants of the workshop, or I could let go and show up calm, relaxed, and in control. I joked with the taxi driver and let go fully. When I arrived late, the people were understanding and welcoming. I was relaxed and ready to perform, we had great session, and I stayed on to make up the time I'd missed. By letting go I could calm my mind, escape my thoughts, and return to the now.

EXERCISE

What situations cause you to overthink the most? Being in a rush? Messaging a friend? Emailing a boss? Setting up a new project? Making decisions? What thought, outcome, or idea are you holding on to? Look for the situations that create repetitive thoughts and feelings and ask yourself:

- **What idea am I holding on to?**
- **What would be different if I let go?**

Attachment and detachment are forms of control. Your mind is a problem-solving machine; it's just that many of the problems it tries to solve are self-created. You try to control others or an outcome by attaching to them, or you try to escape emotional discomfort by detaching altogether.

LENS CHECK

Take a moment to reflect on what life's like for someone who is constantly overthinking everything. They spend hours in their head ruminating about every choice, situation, and project they have, never switching off. What's it like in their mind? How do they see the world? How do they find decisions? How focused are they? How much energy do they have?

Non-attachment allows you to experience fully by letting go of controlling the outcome. This is why people who overthink a lot have trouble getting to sleep at night. I had this problem too, until I realized what happens just before you go to sleep – you let go. When you sleep, you have to trust your body to take over – the autonomic nervous system continues to regulate your heartbeat and your breathing. You don't control this; you let go and the body still works perfectly.

In a similar way, you need to let go of your attachment to thought while you're awake by returning to the present moment. When you're in the here and now, you can trust yourself to take action and start. This means not spending time thinking about what might happen in the future or what happened in the past, but being grounded in the now. If you want to see attachment in its purest form, sit down to meditate. The moment you close your eyes and bring your attention to your breath, your ego will do anything possible to keep you thinking. It will give you great ideas and remind you of important tasks to do, because the moment you start to quieten the mind and focus only on the breath it feels threatened.

This is true for any of your attachments – giving them up feels scary, and your ego will do whatever it can to hold on. This is why you have to start before you're ready because, if it's new, different, or unknown, you need to teach your ego with your actions that you're willing to let go. Starting before you're ready is where the future you and past you collide; you get to choose who wins.

Avoid Replaying the Past

One way we get lost in thought is by focusing on the past and going over it again and again, thinking about what might have been. What if you'd taken a different action? What if things had been different? Often, poker players I work with spend hours replaying past mistakes, thinking about what might have happened if they'd taken more time to think or made a better choice. I used to do this myself until I learned what I'm about to share with you.

Past thinking can generate a lot of frustration and lead to spending a great deal of time doubting your abilities or beating yourself up for not getting it right. It leads to self-blame, which can lead to feeling immobilized in the present. Do you think about the past and wish it could be different? What regrets do you have? What do you wish you had done differently? You carry these memories and frustrations around with you – it's like you're wearing a backpack, and each mistake or regret goes inside it and weighs you down. Holding on to them prevents you from enjoying the present moment.

The reason we do this is to avoid dealing with what we're facing now, in the present. When you're thinking about a mistake you made, you don't have to face what's in front of you right now. It's easier to think about a relationship that went wrong and complain about it than it is to get out dating again. It's easier to think that you shouldn't have hired that person, rather than having an uncomfortable conversation with them about what you'd like to see change. It's easier to say you're in the wrong career or should have studied something different than it is to quit and set up your new business or go back to university.

What I'm about to share with you are a number of truths that, once accepted, will set you free from the past:

1. **You can't change the past.** No amount of thinking about it can change what happened. Wanting it to be different will simply cause you unnecessary suffering. If you made a mistake, you made a mistake. If you lost money, you lost money. If someone betrayed you, they betrayed you.

2. **You couldn't have done anything differently** than you did in the past, ever. You may have had different options at the time, but they were not available to you because you didn't have the awareness to act on them. If you could have done things differently, you would have.

3. **Other people couldn't have done anything differently** from what they did in the past because they were doing the best they could with what they had. Blaming them only hurts you. You can't change or undo what they did and trying to only causes suffering and overthinking.

The moment you choose to accept that you can't change the past, you're free. You'll return to the present ready to take action and enjoy the now.

Don't live in the past, learn from it.

No amount of thinking, wishing, or hoping can change actions you took in the past. When this truth lands for you, it will bring you an immense amount of freedom because anytime you catch yourself wishing you had prepared more, trained more, or made different choices, you can choose to let it all go by reminding yourself that if you could have, you would have. See past rumination as a sign you're avoiding dealing with something in the present and use the lessons from it to help you start now.

Forgive yourself and others

If you find yourself replaying the past, one of the most powerful tools you can use to let it go is forgiveness. Forgiveness isn't about anyone else, it's about you. The pain, anger, frustration, regret, and resentment you carry around is in your backpack, weighing you down. Staying angry at someone else is like holding a hot coal and expecting them to get burned - it only hurts you. The same is true for staying angry at yourself. Forgiveness is a way of closing off the past so it can be put back there, leaving you free to live in the now. The exercise below will talk you through a forgiveness process.

EXERCISE

The past only affects you in the present if you bring it here with you. Ask yourself the following questions to help you to let go of situations from the past that you may have been replaying. It may have been something last week or it may have been 10 years ago - either way, it's time to forgive and let go.

- **What happened and what did I do? What did others do?**
- **What do I wish could be different?**
- **Can I change what happened in the past?**

- **Does thinking about the past make any difference to it?**
- **How does continuing to think about this impact me now?**
- **What do I need to accept or let go of to be free from thinking about it?**
- **What can I learn from it?**
- **Who do I need to forgive?**
- **If I fully forgave this person, what would this do for me?**

You may need to repeat this process if something is still on your mind. Just like acceptance, forgiveness is a process. You may forgive someone and feel free, only for the feelings of frustration to return. That's OK and perfectly normal. Notice the thoughts and feelings, and commit to forgiving again. Forgiveness doesn't remove the memory or erase the past, but it stops it from affecting you now.

A metaphor I always remember comes from Wayne Dyer, who said, 'Nobody ever dies from a snake bite. Once you have been bitten you can't be unbitten, but it is the venom that courses through your veins that causes the damage.' That venom is the anger, resentment, jealousy, and hatred for yourself or others from the past. The venom isn't what happened – that's the bite; the venom is the thoughts you have about the bite that manifest in negative emotions. Forgiveness is the antivenom; it's your path to inner peace and an act of self-love.

Let go for you. And if you can't forgive, then accept. Acceptance is saying, 'It is what it is' and acknowledging that it can't be different or changed. Choose to accept that you were bitten. This choice will stop you ruminating about the past and bring you back to the now, so you can start before you're ready.

Stop projecting the past onto the future

Imagine you're walking through the park and you see a dog running toward you. If you've had a bad experience with a dog in the past – maybe a dog barked loudly and aggressively at you when you were five – your brain will have remembered it and stored it. So, even if this dog is friendly and wags its tail at you, your body reacts like you're in danger. You tense up, your heart races, fear takes over, and you want to run. Your emotional reaction isn't about *this* dog, it's your brain replaying the past experience and projecting into the future, creating a filter for your experience. When you bring awareness to this, you can pause, question your reaction with curiosity, and respond in a way that's more aligned with the reality of the present situation.

Take someone who wants to start a new job – maybe they think, *What if I mess up? What if others don't think I'm good enough?* These worries aren't coming from the new job; they're a reaction learned in the past. If you were criticized in the past for trying something new or judged in school when you made a mistake, then a new job can bring up these concerns. Negative past experiences can lead to associating new beginnings with failure and judgment.

Use the powerful framework below to shine a light on your projections and shift to a space of present-moment clarity.

- **Acknowledge:** Notice the feelings and thoughts you're having without judgment.
- **Accept:** Accept them as feelings and thoughts, not facts.
- **Choose:** Choose what to focus on.
- **Respond:** Take an action aligned with reality, not your projection.

Example

- **Acknowledge:** I'm feeling anxious because I'm projecting my past fear onto my new business.
- **Accept:** This fear comes from a failure in the past but I'm a different person now. It's OK to feel this way.
- **Choose:** I choose to focus on learning from the past, gaining new skills, and being courageous.
- **Respond:** I take a bold action, reach out to a potential client, and share my business online, knowing that the worry is a reaction to the past, not the truth.

Stop Worrying About the Future

Another way we get lost in thought is to drift off into the future – known as 'anticipatory anxiety' or 'future-tripping.' Focusing on the future involves predicting outcomes and worrying what will happen if it doesn't work out how you want it to. Future thinking also involves painting a mental picture in your mind that blows things out of proportion, such as, 'If I give this talk and people don't like it, they'll tell everyone I'm rubbish and my career will be ruined.' Predicting the future is another form of attempting to control what you can't.

Flip the 'what ifs'

One common way we predict the future is through 'what ifs.' For example, 'What if they don't like it?' or 'What if I fail?' or 'What if people get mad at me?' These 'what ifs' are another way we try to create a sense of certainty and control, but they often backfire, leaving us more uncertain and no closer to our goals.

While in heavy traffic a few months back, I wanted to change lanes and I said to my wife, 'What if no one lets me out?' Years ago, I would have stayed with that thought and kept it in my head and stayed in my lane, literally. My 'what if' thoughts predicted the other drivers looking angrily at me, but, after saying it out loud, we both laughed about it. I changed my thought to, *What if people are willing to let me out?* Soon after I indicated, a driver flashed me and a space opened right up. If the initial 'what if' had been left to take up territory in my mind, we could still be sitting in that lane waiting.

What are the 'what ifs' you experience? Use the exercise below to stop the train of thoughts going down the wrong track in your mind and help you switch to a new track.

EXERCISE

Think about a situation that causes you to get stuck in your head. Write down all the 'what ifs' that come up. Now flip each of them from a negative outcome to the outcome you want. For example:

- **'What if my business fails?' flips to 'What if it succeeds?'**
- **'What if no one likes my post?' flips to 'What if it goes viral?'**
- **'What if I can't handle it?' flips to 'What if I enjoy it?'**

Now see which direction your mind goes in. You've turned a negative thought you may have ruminated on into a positive thought you can act upon. This is the power of self-awareness and choosing your thoughts. You choose the direction of your mind and your life. Anytime you catch yourself predicting a negative future, stop the 'what if' and flip it. This is a genuinely life-changing practice.

The above exercise is powerful for a number of reasons. First off, it might save you hours spent in negative rumination, overthinking the scenarios you don't want. Secondly, it will get you focused on what you *do* want and, as we've seen, what you focus on is what expands. Thirdly, you'll find that, with enough practice, you actually start to like or look forward to the thing you either disliked or were afraid of. Back this up with a positive affirmation such as 'I'm looking forward to...' or 'I can't wait to...' or 'It's going to go well' and you'll stop worrying about the future and rewire your mind for the positive.

Get grounded in reality

Anytime you're lost in thoughts about the future, you're off in your imagination and habitual ways of thinking and not grounded in the reality of the present moment. Let's break down thought and reality in a quick example, so you can clearly see when you're lost in thought versus dealing with reality:

Your boss calls, but you miss it = **reality**.

Your boss calls, you miss it, and you think, *My boss doesn't usually call me. I'll give them a call back in the morning to see what it's about* = **thinking about reality**.

Your boss calls, you miss it, and you think, *My boss never calls me, they usually email. What the hell? Am I going to get fired? Do I need to start working on my resume? Have I done anything wrong lately?* Then you stay in this pattern of thought all evening and struggle to sleep = **overthinking about reality**.

Thinking = productive and moves you into action.

Overthinking = unproductive and halts you from taking action.

The call from your boss is a fact, it's real, and the rest is all thought – predictions and assumptions about what *might* happen that you cannot be certain *will* happen. Yet, when you aren't aware of this, you may begin to merge your thoughts with the fact and then start reacting to it. You're always reacting to your *thinking* about reality and not reality itself. This is a key concept I invite you to see: *You react to your thoughts about the facts, not the facts themselves.*

Maybe your boss doesn't call you often so it prompts some suspicion, but everything you add to the fact is a prediction about the future and not fact. How you use these predictions determines the quality of your life and your ability to start before you're ready. If you make endless negative predictions, it will feel like you've failed before you've even started. You'll think yourself out of action. By seeing the illusion of these predictions, you can choose to view starting as something exciting and step into the unknown with faith.

We all get creative with our thinking – thinking is a gift and is what gives life meaning. It's just that sometimes we get a little too creative and our own creations start to run us. This is the power of thought, and when there's too much thought and too little awareness, that power works against you. This is the true cost of overthinking.

Ask yourself, 'What is fact and what am I assuming?' If it's an assumption, it's not true. This means you're adding to the facts. For example, 'I'm going to be late for my meeting' is the fact and 'I'm going to be late for my meeting *and* people are going to hate me and I'll be fired' is the assumption. It's the second part of the sentence that fires up your imagination and makes your mind race.

Practice sticking with the facts and pausing your assumptions to ground yourself in reality.

Escape the Holding Pattern

When you get lost in overthinking, you may get stuck in holding patterns in different areas of your life, stuck in a state of waiting or rumination, like a plane circling an airport without landing. It occurs when you're not making progress toward your goals, either due to external circumstances or internal hesitations. On a macro scale, this can look like staying in a job or relationship that no longer aligns with your goals and values but not taking any steps to change it. On a micro scale, it can look like not texting a friend back because you're obsessing about the right thing to say.

Holding patterns are attachment in action – they're your ego's attempt to protect you from feeling emotional pain, losing control, and facing uncertainty by holding on to a thought, person, goal, or situation. It's an attempt at control. The possibility of experiencing failure, embarrassment, judgment, rejection, uncomfortable feelings you'd rather avoid, or expending energy can trigger a holding pattern. Holding patterns also try to protect you from losing control – over your time, money, energy, or possessions – and uncertainty: the fear of stepping into the unknown and leaving the safety of what feels familiar. Although, on the surface, holding patterns appear to keep you safe, they also keep you stuck, which results in continued overthinking, fear, and inaction.

When in a holding pattern, you're stuck in a survival state of overthinking and waiting for the 'perfect time' to act, rather than moving forward with imperfect conditions. This might make you feel safe temporarily, but leads to missed opportunities and increases the fear of starting. The longer you stay there, the more fearful you become. The key to breaking free forever is understanding the thinking that's going on in your head.

I used to do anything to avoid being stuck with my inner thoughts because they were so relentless and mean to me. That was until I understood that the thoughts were not actually me, and I distinguished who and what the thoughts were and what they were trying to achieve. There are two voices you can listen to: The first can be problematic when it takes up too much airtime; the second holds the key to breaking free from holding patterns and overthinking. The first voice is your inner critic.

Your inner critic

Your inner critic is the voice you recorded from your parents or carers growing up – it's your ego. You may hear the musts, shoulds, and rules it wants you to follow. It wants control through order, routine, structure, and being right.

The goal of your inner critic is to keep you safe. It wants you to succeed at all costs and so tries to ensure you'll never fail. It wants to solve problems, make sure you look good, and maintain a sense of control. Despite its good intentions, the inner critic often manifests in perfectionism, people-pleasing, and procrastination – and it comes from a place of fear.

The critic uses harsh self-talk, judgment, and criticism to motivate you. It tries to shame you into action, highlights your mistakes, and demands success, structure, and rules. Due to its need to avoid failure, nothing will ever be good enough. This can leave you in a spiral of overthinking, trying to meet its demands.

The inner critic gets louder when you're about to do something where you might fail or risk being criticized. If you listen to it, then you go back to your safe space and stay in the holding pattern where it holds on through attachment. Not listening to it is like giving away your favorite item of clothing - you may think you'll be lost without it, but, after fully letting go, you can see you didn't need it to be happy.

I can tell you with total certainty that distinguishing my inner critic from who I really am is one of the most life-changing tools I've ever practiced. I used to overthink a lot, spend weeks ruminating on past decisions and events, and worry about the future. When I realized that the critic isn't me, but instead is a part of me that tries to keep me safe, I discovered that I didn't have to listen to it. I could use it and not have it use me. The critic needs to think to survive, which is why it's so attached to thought. When you get silent, you access another part of you that contains more wisdom, clarity, and freedom...

Your inner self

Your inner self is the voice of your higher self - it's your inner wisdom, awareness, intuition, and ideas. It's your adult present self, free from fear, judgment, and distorted thinking.

Your inner self lives in the present with purpose, passion, and authenticity. It wants you to experience your highest expression and reach your full potential. It comes from a place of love.

Its sole focus is to expand, to help you do what you love and love who you are. It works on living your purpose, staying in the present, and focusing on the process. These all take you out of thinking about the past or the future and into the now, where you move with intention.

When the inner critic is driving you, you'll stay in a never-ending stream of thoughts and 'what ifs.' When you listen to your inner self instead, trust your intuition, and take action, you prove to your critic that you're capable of surviving failures and setbacks, that you can let go and survive. You can spend 10 seconds, 10 minutes, 10 months, or 10 years in a holding pattern depending on how clearly you see and distinguish your inner critic thoughts from your inner self. This is why the journey of starting before you're ready is a lifelong one – you can't get rid of your inner critic; instead, you need to learn to act while it's there.

Get out of your head

Breaking out of a holding pattern in one area of your life provides immense opportunities to carry this courage, awareness, and confidence into other areas too. As you apply what you learn here, you can expect to experience multiple breakthroughs of emotional and mental freedom. Distinguishing the inner critic gives you freedom and clarity, because you can choose to hear the voice and take action anyway. In acceptance and commitment therapy (ACT), this is called 'self-as-context,' where you see your thoughts as not who you really are – you're the one observing them. This puts you back in the driver's seat, so you don't have to get lost in your head.

Often, when you're closest to a breakthrough, the inner critic gets really loud – it wants to hold on, to stay attached to what it believes because this keeps it alive. It's your job to show it that you've got this. Your critic will use emotions to keep you in line and this is why you often don't *feel* ready – the overthinking is a cover-up for this, a distraction to keep you attached, circling, and not starting. When you're willing to let go of your inner critic and start before you're ready, you're aligning with your inner self.

The inner critic is trying to help you in some way, to maintain your boundaries, protect you, keep you safe, and preserve your identity and self-image. It demands a perceived sense of safety and control. When I notice the critic judging or worrying, I separate myself from it mentally through non-attachment. Initially, this took some effort, but over time, many of the mental patterns drop off as they lose their power when you don't react to them. Attachment is when the critic runs you – you're convinced that if you're late you'll be fired, if you tell your friend the truth they'll hate you, and if you start that project you'll fail. The critic believes it is right. Detachment is when you ignore the critic altogether and pretend it isn't there, saying, 'I don't get scared' or 'It's easy,' or you just avoid starting altogether. Non-attachment allows you to hear the critic but choose whether you listen to it or not.

It's when you're on new ground that you need to bring more awareness to your inner critic and kill it with kindness and compassion. By avoiding action, you feel shielded from the discomfort of failure, fear, judgment, or the unknown. It might give you the illusion of being in control or protect you from immediate discomfort, but this perceived safety and comfort is temporary and keeps you from moving toward your true goals. The cost of listening to the critic rather than your own wisdom is missed opportunities, stagnation, unrealized potential, and, ultimately, anxiety. The longer you remain in a holding pattern, the greater the consequences become: You lose precious time and delay your progress toward your goals. This is why people often take action when they've had enough and reached a breaking point. You don't have to wait until this point - change can happen now because you can start before you're ready.

EXERCISE

What's something that causes you to go into a holding pattern of overthinking? It might be making sales calls at work, going to the gym, a past relationship, posting on social media, writing a book, taking up a new hobby, or starting anything new.

Ask yourself the following questions:

- **What does my inner critic say to me?**
- **How is it trying to help me? How is it holding me back?**
- **What is it holding on to? What does it want?**
- **What does listening to it cost me?**
- **What does my inner self want? What do I really want?**

Recognizing when you're in a holding pattern allows you to break free from your attachments, stopping you from repeating the cycles of overthinking and self-sabotage. You can instead take action, even if the conditions aren't perfect and even when you don't feel ready. This is the game. When you're no longer a prisoner of your thoughts, you're free to take action, knowing you can trust your inner self and not the inner critic's thoughts that are trying to keep you safe.

Act on Your Insights

I was sitting on a tiny sofa with my girlfriend's dad in our one-bedroom flat in Surrey, feeling very nervous. My girlfriend was in the shower; I could hear it running from where we were sitting. I'd been dating her for less than a year and her dad was visiting from America. As we sat on the sofa talking, I knew that I wanted to ask his permission for her to marry me. He would be over for a few weeks, and I thought I could ask him later, but then I remembered a tool I had learned from Mel Robbins called the five-second rule. It's really simple and you can use it to get out of overthinking and into action. You simply count down from five to one and, when you get to one, you take action without thinking about it too much.

As the fear welled up in me and I started painting scenarios of her dad shouting at me and thinking I should wait for a better time, I started the countdown: Five, four, three, two, one... and spoke: 'Hey Ed, can I ask you a question?' It was too late to turn back. To my delight, he said 'yes.' I could have spent the next two weeks ruminating on this, waiting for the perfect time, planning it out, thinking about it, and, knowing me, talking myself out of it. Instead, I took action.

This tool will help you to outsmart your inner critic and avoid negotiating with your ego. Where can you use the five-second rule to get out of your head and into action? Maybe you want to get out of bed and to the gym; maybe you have a sales call to make; maybe you want to express yourself with some friends. Count down from five and, when you get to one, put your thoughts to one side and take action. Do it before you're ready. You can stay in your head, or you can get out and live your life – it's your call.

The pessimist thinks the glass is half empty.
The optimist thinks the glass is half full.
The inspired action-taker drinks the water.

Change Your State

One of the best ways to step out of overthinking and escape your inner critic is to change your state of mind. Your state of mind is your attitude, mood, and focus in any given moment, and you can shift it by changing what you focus on and what you do with your body.

The mind and body are connected, hence the term 'psychosomatic,' with 'psyche' being the mind and 'soma' being the body. The way you think affects the way you feel, and the way you move your body affects the thoughts in your mind.

Move your body

Adopting a confident posture for just a couple of minutes can have a profound impact on your mindset and body. Standing tall with your chest open, hands on your hips or arms raised overhead, can signal to your brain that you're in control. This posture not only jolts you out of unwanted thought patterns, it boosts your energy levels and helps calm the physiological effects of stress. When you feel more empowered and less stressed, you're far more likely to take decisive action, even in moments of uncertainty.

Some other ways to change your physiology and shift your state of mind are to stand up, move around, switch rooms, take a shower, or splash cold water on your face. Ask yourself, 'How do I want to feel?' Then go and do something that makes you feel that way, such as going for a run or a walk, or calling a friend and telling them you appreciate them. What you do changes how you feel, and vice versa!

Move your mind

As we've explored, when you're overthinking, you may be lost in thought or stuck in a holding pattern. Change your focus to break the pattern. You can move from being tangled up in the thoughts inside your mind to becoming aware of your thoughts and the observer of them. The moment you notice and label your thoughts, you're no longer attached to them. Try saying to yourself, 'I'm lost in overthinking again' and, without judgment, celebrate this awareness. Each time you catch yourself overthinking, you're one step closer to being free of it.

Choose where to place your attention. Ask yourself, 'What am I focusing on?' This question will interrupt overthinking by bringing your awareness to it, like someone tapping you on the shoulder and waking you up. Then ask, 'What would I like to focus my attention on instead?' If you're focused on worrying, choose instead to focus on being grateful, or your values, or your purpose. Sitting down and doing a short five-minute meditation can be enough to quieten the excess thinking in your mind (try the short guided meditation in Chapter 6, *page 139*). When you get out of your head and into action regularly, your thoughts will be like clouds in the sky – you don't worry about them, you just notice them and let them float on by.

LENS CHECK

Take a moment to reflect on what life's like for someone who is present and focused, who spends more time in action than in their head. How do they experience their personal and professional life? They switch off when they feel the need to and see their thoughts as passing clouds they don't have to engage with unless they want to. They have learned not to be ruled by their inner critic and instead have a calm and deep trust in themselves. How connected are they to their inner truth and wisdom? What role does their inner self play when starting something new? How do they feel about themselves?

Starting before you're ready is reminding yourself that you won't feel different later – the unhelpful thoughts and doubts won't always go away, and the inner critic won't disappear because it's inside your head. Instead of staying in your head, listening to the inner critic and never taking action, access your inner self and remember that you don't need anything else to get started - you're ready now. It will feel scary at first, but the critic will get quieter and, over time, you'll become more connected with who you really are. You'll become great at starting before you're ready.

We'll now meet and take down impostor syndrome - a close relative of overthinking. As you bring awareness to these unhelpful thinking habits and transform them, you'll become free to start doing what you love.

KEY TAKEAWAYS

- **Let go of holding on to the past through the process of acceptance and forgiveness. Choose to accept what has happened and focus on being here in the present moment.**
- **Distinguish your inner critic from your inner self. As you begin to turn the volume down on your ego, you'll listen to and act from your true self.**
- **Get out of your head and into action by moving your body and shifting your focus to break free from the overthinking trap.**

CHAPTER 5

Combat Impostor Syndrome

Imagine you were hypnotized to believe that everyone else in the world knows exactly what you know. You now believe that all the skills you have, which took you years to practice and master, everyone else could easily do. All your qualifications, which took years of hard work for you to acquire, anyone else could easily achieve. All the knowledge you have learned, everyone else already knows. What would that feel like for you?

Maybe you'd feel like all your hard work wasn't so hard. Maybe you'd feel like all your successes weren't really that impressive. Even though you're an expert, it might feel like you're simply a beginner, just starting out. Maybe you'd play down your achievements and maybe you wouldn't bother sharing them with others because, well, they were so easy to achieve, anyone could have done it. Maybe you'd feel like a fraud and that at any moment, someone might tap you on the shoulder and say, 'Look buddy, the game's up – we know you're a fake, we've found you out.' You'd spend your whole life working hard and striving for success yet feeling anxious and never really enjoying it. This is what impostor syndrome feels like and, in this chapter, I'll offer some easy ways to help you confront that impostor and unleash the free, fun, and bold version of you.

What Is Impostor Syndrome?

I've lived most of my life feeling like an impostor. It's that horrible feeling that, deep down, you're just not good enough, so you keep working harder and harder to try to make that feeling go away, but it never does. Impostor syndrome is caused by thinking that other people know more than they do and that you know less than you do. It's a warped perception of yourself and your abilities, coupled with that belief we saw in Chapter 1 – that you're not good enough. When you feel like an impostor, new opportunities terrify you, as they're a chance for you to get exposed as a fraud, so you hesitate at the thought of starting something, making changes or bold moves, or putting yourself out there.

You don't want to take risks because people might find out that you don't really know what you're talking about, so you avoid being proactive or reaching out to people to offer your services or help and, instead, you play it safe. You look back at the work you've done and think either it's not that great or that anyone could have done it, and so you keep trying to perfect what you've done or look for the new best thing you could learn that will finally make you feel like you know what you're doing.

You constantly compare yourself to people who are 'better' than you or at the very top of their career, and this makes starting new tasks feel daunting. You miss out on celebrating your wins and you don't recognize your accomplishments. The sad truth about impostor syndrome is that you're the only person in your life who can't see your greatness. It's the thing that keeps you inches away from fulfilling your potential. Now it's time to close that gap.

Where does it come from?

Impostor syndrome is primarily driven by how you compare yourself to others and evaluate your abilities and capabilities as much lower than they really are. When this gets fueled with perfectionism, it can become a real block to feeling good about yourself, having high self-confidence, and starting anything new. The unknown becomes the very place where you might get exposed and the idea of making mistakes and receiving criticism or judgment triggers your inner feelings of being a fraud.

A new business opportunity, meeting new people, or a new relationship can all be situations where you could get 'found out,' but only when you believe the lies that impostor syndrome tries to feed you. Impostor syndrome is also triggered by fear, and fear isn't something that's going to go away if you want to keep growing. Author and coach Rich Litvin said, 'Stop trying to get rid of impostor syndrome. And start getting good at it.'

LENS CHECK

Take a moment to reflect on what life's like for someone who is the world's biggest impostor, who doubts themselves at every turn. How fearful are they about new opportunities? How do they feel about themselves? They don't see their value and think they need to do more to feel capable, so they hide themselves. How much self-trust do they have? How much of their value are they missing out on?

You can't remove your doubts and fear altogether, but by understanding where your impostor feelings come from and putting your knowledge and skill set into its proper place, you can gain mastery over these feelings and start treating yourself like someone who deserves to have the success you've created, and enjoy the success you're about to create.

It's Time to Be the Pilot

I spent a lot of my life holding back and waiting for my turn. My lack of self-worth created by my own impostor syndrome meant that I didn't put myself out there and often avoided the spotlight. I didn't want to risk standing on stage and having everyone see right through me. As a result, I played everything down: I played down my strengths, my accomplishments, and even my relationships, thinking that people probably didn't like me as much as they did. As I practiced many of the tools in this book and expanded my comfort zone, I built my confidence day by day and tried new things, like improv comedy and public speaking. I joined a toastmaster's club and started to speak to groups of people, which really helped me build my confidence and also make myself visible – there's no hiding on stage.

One evening, I was given the role of toastmaster. This role requires you to host the evening. As I got up, I launched into my opening speech and shared that it was my first time as toastmaster and asked the people attending to go easy on me. I didn't realize it at the time, but this was impostor syndrome speaking: 'Don't big yourself up too much, you might fall.'

The evening went well; I introduced the speakers, kept it fun and flowing on time, there was a great atmosphere, and people enjoyed it. At the end of the evening, a guest from another club evaluates the speakers and gives feedback to everyone, including the toastmaster. She said that I'd done an excellent job; however, she had a recommendation for me to improve. She said, 'If you were to get on a plane and the pilot was to come on board and say, "Afternoon everyone, welcome to the flight. Just to let you know it's my first-ever flight today, so go easy on me," how would you feel?' People want to feel like they're in safe hands, and playing the role of an impostor is watering yourself down as self-protection. By saying it was my first time, I was giving an excuse early in case I failed, instead of acting with confidence and courage, and backing myself to succeed.

The next time I played the role of toastmaster, I showed up in a different way. I prepared beforehand and when it was time to introduce myself, I said, 'Hey everyone, welcome to the evening. You're in safe hands tonight; I'm here to make sure the evening flows smoothly, so any problems, come and see me and I'll take care of it.' As we touched on in Chapter 1, when stepping into new situations, you're going to have times when you don't know if you'll succeed, you might not feel certain, or you may be doing something for the first time (maybe even flying your first plane...). It will bring up the impostor feelings. But everyone has to take their first flight, or have their first day on the job, or make the first move. You can do it as an impostor, or you can step into the version of you who can.

Decide you're ready now

When you change how you see yourself, you treat yourself differently and the world around you responds to this. Think about the thing you want to start and say, 'I'm ready to go and do it now; I'm worthy of doing it.' How does it feel to say that? Do you feel empowered? Or do you notice some impostor feelings creeping up? The key is to not react to those feelings and play small, but instead make a decision that you're up to the task and play the role of the person who can do it.

If you're flying a plane, it's because you've completed your training and you're ready to go. If you're being toastmaster, it's because you've been at the club speaking for a number of months and are ready to lead. If you're writing a book, it's because you have something important to say and it's time to share it with the world. You need to allow yourself to feel important and worthy enough to take the steps and make it happen. Use the mantra 'I am worthy of being here' to remind yourself that you have importance and value, whether you feel like an impostor or not. Feeling deserving of taking the step isn't the same as entitlement. Feeling worthy is saying you deserve to have a shot at the table; entitlement is saying that because you worked hard or put yourself out there, you deserve to win – and it's a trap. There's no guarantee of success, but there is a guarantee that you'll build confidence and self-worth by no longer acting like an impostor and not starting, and taking bold steps as a leader instead. When you make being ready a decision, not a feeling you wait for, you'll be ready to act the part now.

The Four Levels of Competence

No matter what talent you have, everyone starts at the beginning when doing something new – there's a learning curve that we all follow. It can require effort and feel uncomfortable, but it's a natural process we all go through. You can't skip starting as a beginner. Learning any new skill follows four separate stages. Let's look at the example of learning to drive a car:

Stage 1: Unconscious incompetence

You don't know what you don't know.

You decide you want to learn to drive but have no idea how much you have to learn. You might think it's relatively simple: just hold the wheel and put your foot on the accelerator.

At this stage, you have no clue what skills you need or that some of them even exist. You're unaware. I was unaware that I could have confidence as I didn't realize I could shift my thoughts and change my actions to build confidence from within. As your awareness rises in any area, you can see the path to mastery; it's no secret. Right now, you may have the potential to be great at many things you don't yet know; maybe playing the piano, a sport, or launching a business or podcast. Use your imagination: What would you love to do?

Stage 2: Conscious incompetence

You know what you don't know.

After your first few driving lessons, it dawns on you just how much there is to learn. You struggle coordinating the clutch, the gears, brakes, and steering, as well as looking in the mirrors, learning the road signs, and navigating other drivers. As you stall the car, you think, *Others make this look easier than it is.*

At stage 2, you become aware of what you don't know. This can be exciting yet also overwhelming, as you see all you have to do to improve. This is where impostor syndrome, anxiety, and doubt kick in. This phase is where you don't *feel* ready and are susceptible to fear, overwhelm, and procrastination. You may think, *Why is this so easy for everyone else?* or *It shouldn't be this hard!* You can feel frustrated and want to learn faster or skip this stage, but by building your tolerance to the frustration, you can master this stage and become a super-learner.

It's incredibly liberating to know that all the feelings in this stage are normal: the frustration, the doubt, even the impostor feelings; we all feel them. By using the tools and knowledge you gain from this book, you'll be equipped to master this stage and stay in the game when you don't feel ready.

Stage 3: Conscious competence

You know, but you have to think about it.

You start to improve with practice and you can drive, but it requires intense focus and determination. You consciously think about changing gears, your speed, and how to do a three-point turn. It can be tiring in this phase.

Stage 3 is where you build the skills and practice, and you start getting better at the thing!

Stage 4: Unconscious competence

You don't have to think about it.

You now have enough experience and skill that driving becomes second nature. You no longer have to think about each action; they happen automatically. You can have a conversation while driving. You may even go a few minutes while driving and wonder how you got there as your subconscious did the driving for you, just as you've trained it to.

So many people drop out too soon, when, if they'd just stayed in the game long enough, they could have reached this final stage. At stage 4, the skills become second nature; you can do them in your sleep. It takes far less effort and you can learn other new tasks on top of this.

If you're willing to experience some frustration, accept it's normal, and keep going, you could master anything you choose to. You'll advance through these levels in many skills throughout your life, but remember: You have to start at stage 1 each time – we all do and that's OK.

Change Your Perception

Even though at times you might feel like a fraud, other people don't know what you know. All the skills you've spent years learning and building are unique to you. You had to go through the four levels of competence to build them, so own them. No one else in the world has your skill set, knowledge, and experience because no one has walked your path. That means that you have something no one else has, and this makes you immensely valuable, rare, and helpful to others.

Many people take on impostor syndrome from their parents while growing up, or by watching others playing themselves down or being overly modest – we record these behaviors in our subconscious and take them on for ourselves. The role of an impostor is often learned and you can unlearn it with patience and practice. If you can be hypnotized to believe you are an impostor, like many of us in childhood, you can also be un-hypnotized.

It's time to see yourself as successful, accomplished, and worthy of success.

A new opportunity isn't a chance to be found out; it's a chance to show people what you can do and to prove to yourself that you can do it. If you're in business, bring your skill set to the table – all the books you've read, courses you've taken, and knowledge you have is inside of you and people need it, so start. If you want to create a new relationship, you have a whole host of fun, love, and excitement to bring to someone else; don't deny them of it.

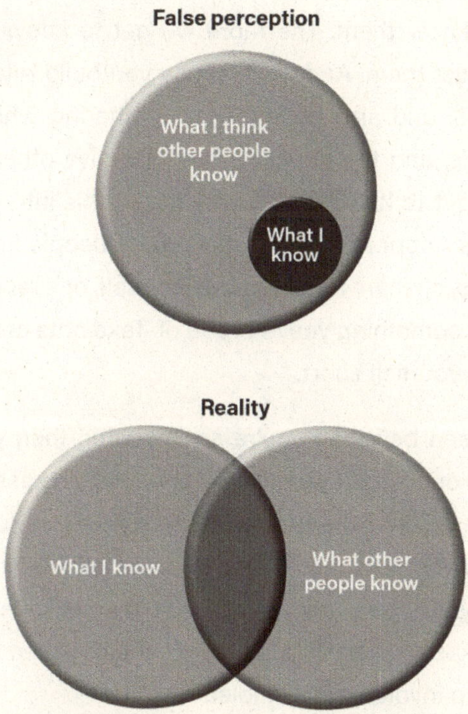

Figure 1: Impostor Syndrome – Perception vs. Reality

If you don't share what you know, then others won't find out and you'll be less likely to start and create new opportunities for yourself. You also won't be able to offer your services to others if you're a business, or add value to other peoples' lives by sharing your gifts. Imagine being in a room with Cristiano Ronaldo and you don't know who he is. When you ask what he does for a living, he says, 'I play a little football here and there; it's no big deal,' and then he changes the conversation. You'd have no idea that he has won major trophies and inspired millions of children to take up sport and play a game they love.

Context is key: The more we know about someone, the more we get to know them. The more we get to know them, the more we trust them. And trust is how you build relationships, connections, and also confidence. By sharing who you are, what you do, and the impact it has, you give other people a chance to get to know you. A way to put this into practice is to take every opportunity you have to let people know about what you do, or share a story about yourself, or a recent or past success, or something you're proud of. Take note of where you tend to sell yourself short.

If you've been believing you're an impostor, then you'll have discounted or downplayed all your previous successes, so you might have missed them or written them off as luck. You're not alone; even the great Albert Einstein felt like an impostor and once said, 'The exaggerated esteem in which my lifework is held makes me very ill at ease. I feel compelled to think of myself as an involuntary swindler.'

Missing your success would be like climbing Everest and saying you just went for a stroll up a little hill – you'd miss out on gaining confidence from recognizing what you're capable of.

It's time to acknowledge your successes. Make sure you don't skip over this exercise – it's an important part of banishing those impostor thoughts.

EXERCISE

Write down everything you've accomplished up until this point: your education, awards, qualifications, life and career successes - no matter how big or small you think they are. As you create this list, walk back through your successes mentally - this is the fuel that will feed your confidence for when you next need to start before you're ready.

Next, something I learned from author and coach Steve Chandler is to create a success file: Gather supportive, complimentary, or appreciative emails from colleagues, clients, friends, and family. Collate all the positive feedback, testimonials, reviews, and comments you've received from others. Reflect on these when you feel self-doubt and impostor syndrome rising or when it's time to step on new soil and start before you're ready. Reminding yourself of the positive impact you've made is a great way to build your self-esteem when you need a boost.

Drop the False Humility

Playing down your skills and achievements too much is a false sense of humility that comes as a side effect of impostor syndrome. Real humility is being grounded, open-minded, and self-aware. False humility is really a form of self-protection, where you fear bigging yourself up too much to avoid getting knocked down and having a harder fall. It's a disguised form of pride, where self-deprecation or playing down your strengths is used as a way to gain approval, appear modest, or avoid criticism. When you shift to real humility, you're able to see your own greatness and the greatness that lies in others beneath their own impostor facades.

Ask yourself, 'Why am I not putting myself out there? Why am I being humble?' Be honest with yourself as you answer these questions. If the answer is 'To stay grounded and present,' then great, but if the answer is based in fear, such as, 'I'm scared people will think I'm arrogant' or 'What if I say I can do it and I can't?' then it's time to give yourself permission to step into your greatness. Allow yourself to feel worthy. Author and speaker Marianne Williamson said, 'Our deepest fear is not that we are inadequate. Our deepest fear is that we are powerful beyond measure.' When my daughter says, 'Daddy, look at this picture I just drew!' I don't think she's being arrogant, I think she's genuinely proud of what she created, and I celebrate with her – and it feels great for both of us. We aren't born to hide; we're born to be ourselves, be seen, to express our gifts and talents, and share them with the world.

Be proud of what you've created and be proud of who you are – the world needs your gifts.

Share your successes

Here's how to put this into practice: For the next week, refuse to put yourself down or play down your skills and achievements as luck. No more saying, 'Oh, that's just little old me,' or 'I play football but I'm not that great,' or 'I don't usually do this well.' Don't allow yourself even to joke about your shortcomings.

Talk about your strengths, share them with others, offer your services, and tell people about your wins. Share the facts of what you've achieved – there's no arrogance in a fact, it's the truth. If you say, 'I was top of my class,' that's a fact and we can all appreciate that. If you say, 'I was top of my class and that makes me better than everyone else,' that's another story. You can be humble and own your successes. You'll be amazed at how this starts to tame the impostor in you and fire up your inner confidence.

When you share your wins with others, your brain experiences a surge of dopamine, serotonin, and oxytocin. Dopamine is the reward chemical in the brain and, when it's released, it can boost your motivation levels, reinforcing feelings of progress and success. Serotonin is linked to status, pride, and belonging, and, when you share your success, you signal to your brain and others that you're worthy of it. Oxytocin is the connection chemical and, when sharing wins with a friend, partner, or coach, you increase feelings of trust and belonging. And here's the cool thing: The same happens for the people listening to you. When hearing about your successes, mirror neurons activate in the other person, making them feel inspired, proud, and more connected to you.

Below is an exercise that will reduce the impostor and build your inner courage.

EXERCISE

Every day – either first thing in the morning or at the end of the day – grab your journal and write down three things

you're proud of yourself for. This 'win journal' will help you to pause and reflect on your success. The key is to remember that your brain won't do this for you. Creating this ritual will train your brain to see the steps you're taking and the progress you're making.

As I've allowed myself to appreciate my successes and abilities, I've found myself noticing other people's successes and abilities too, and I make sure to acknowledge them when I see them. When you see a server in a restaurant doing a good job, tell them, 'I really appreciate how friendly you've been; you made us feel welcome and the service today has been exceptional.' When you see your partner succeed, tell them, 'Thanks so much for cooking dinner tonight; it was delicious – you're a great cook.' When you see a client or colleague have a win, celebrate with them: 'I think your accomplishment is extraordinary and I want to acknowledge the hard work you've put in to achieve it.' You never know who feels like an impostor. (Hint: It's more people than you think.)

Celebrate effort

As well as celebrating your wins and successes, it's also important to celebrate effort. Carol Dweck introduced two types of mindset we can fall into in her book *Mindset*: a fixed mindset and a growth mindset. With a fixed mindset, you see your abilities, talents, and personality as something you're born with that can't be changed. A growth mindset is the belief that these aspects of you can be changed and developed through effort, learning, and hard work. When praising your success, remember also to praise the effort that led to that success. Rather than just saying to yourself, 'Congrats on the promotion,' you could say, 'Congrats on the hard work you put in to get that promotion.' If you just celebrate the result, it can lead to a fixed mindset where you see 'you' as great and discount the effort. When praising the effort, you see the 'effort' as what led to the result.

Dweck and her team gave a group of children puzzles to solve and gave them two types of feedback: praise for intelligence ('You must be really smart') and praise for effort ('You must have worked really hard'). They found that those who were praised for effort were more likely to choose more difficult puzzles when given the choice, and those praised for intelligence chose easier tasks. The children praised for effort also maintained motivation and persistence when the puzzles got tough, while those praised for intelligence became discouraged much quicker. The effort-praised children also outperformed those praised for intelligence.[1]

Develop a belief in your ability to grow through hard work and focus, on starting before you're ready and not having to already be an expert, which, yet again, leads to those impostor feelings.

The power of 'yet'

While building a growth mindset, Dweck also identified that it can be helpful to use the word 'yet.' When taking on a new

1 Dweck, C.S. (2016), *Mindset: The New Psychology of Success*. New York: Ballantine Books.

task, project, or venture, it can be easy to say, 'I can't do this,' but the truth is you can't do this *yet* because it's a skill you're learning. Taking on this mindset and having 'yet' in your tool kit will help you see yourself as a work in progress rather than having the pressure of needing to be the finished product now.

While you're complete as a spiritual being and you're enough as you are, your skills are never going to be perfect. Mastery is a road without an end – there's no perfect speaker, footballer, parent, salesperson, or friend. The most enlightened among us know that the more you know, the more there is to learn, so take the pressure off yourself and use the word 'yet' as a reminder that you're always learning and growing:

- 'I can't do it... yet.'
- 'I'm not good at it... yet.'
- 'I'm not an expert... yet.'

Stop Comparing Yourself to Others

One thing that ramps up impostor syndrome is comparing yourself to others. Social comparison was first described by psychologist Leon Festinger in 1954, when he suggested that we have an innate drive to evaluate our abilities relative to others, especially when objective standards are unclear. When we don't know how far along we are, we look to others and this can create unhealthy timeline comparisons, such as, 'They're married and I'm single,' 'They're making six figures with their business and I'm only just setting up my website,' or 'They have 10,000 followers and I only have 500.'

Similar to judgment, social comparison is an automatic process, so don't expect it to never happen and don't beat yourself up when it does – it's how you respond that matters. When your brain automatically judges, you can practice non-judgment by pausing to observe the thought without reacting, acknowledging it with curiosity rather than criticism, and gently redirecting your focus to understanding rather than labeling. When your brain automatically compares, it's time to practice non-comparison. What someone else has is simply different, not better or worse than you. If you didn't compare what you have to them, better wouldn't exist – better only exists in comparison and you get to choose what you focus on.

As you see an influencer online with more followers or a bigger house, your brain may ask, 'Why don't I have that already?' The perfect way to counter this comparison is with gratitude. Focus on what you do have and what you've achieved already, and it will ground you in what you have, not what you lack. See comparison as something that fuels the impostor fire and gratitude as the water that puts it out – it will be one of the most powerful tools in your tool kit to overcoming the impostor trap and boosting self-confidence. Ask yourself, 'What am I grateful for in this moment?' List three things in your mind and really immerse yourself in them; you'll feel great.

Alongside gratitude, there are a few other proven strategies you can use to maintain self-confidence and overcome the impostor feelings. The first is to practice comparing your present self with your past self. Instead of comparing yourself to others or to the person at the top of their game, focus on where you were five years ago. Ask yourself, 'What progress have I made since then and what new skills and knowledge do I have now?' Don't put others above or below you. When I stopped putting the people I admired on a pedestal, I started thinking, *If they can do it, so can I*. This had a profound impact on my confidence and motivation levels. No one is better than you as a person, some people just spend more time building skills than you - you can do that too. Next, focus on getting better each day. Progress is a great motivator and when you focus on measuring effort and areas you can control, you'll make it possible to make regular progress.

Another strategy is to take some time away from social media. We live in a world where people post curated highlight reels of their life and airbrushed photos of themselves with filters galore, and it has created a false view of how others are living. We've always compared ourselves to others, it goes way back; it's just that, in today's world, that comparison has become magnified to a whole new level. There'll always be someone with more skills, more results, more qualifications, or more money than you. Each time a billionaire builds and launches their new super yacht, another billionaire is building and launching an even bigger, better, and more expensive model. Stay focused on your next steps.

Some tips to switch off from social media that I recommend to my clients include:

- Turn off notifications for apps that are not a priority for you.
- Move apps that don't support your well-being or goals off your home screen.

- Set time limits around when you'll use social media and be intentional with why you're using it, who you follow, and why. Practice not using social media in the first and last hour of your day – you'll become more intentional and focused.
- Take a social media detox. Try taking a week off social media to focus on your life and do things you enjoy. This will give you time to focus on what you think and feel and you'll spend less time comparing yourself to others.

You're not alone

Everyone feels uncomfortable on new ground and many still feel like a fraud after years of hard work, success, and accolades. Just like Einstein, many other top performers experience impostor feelings. When I first discovered I wasn't alone in my feelings, I felt like a huge weight had been lifted off my shoulders. David Bowie, Serena Williams, Lady Gaga, Kate Winslet, Ryan Reynolds, and Tom Hanks have all spoken about experiencing impostor syndrome at points in their career. Any new role, environment, or transition can trigger the feelings. After coaching highly successful athletes, business owners, CEOs, influencers, and coaches, I'm going to go out on a limb and say that 100 percent of people experience impostor feelings, yet 90 percent of people are really good at hiding them.

One practice that can really help you to transform impostor syndrome is to share how you feel with someone you trust. This can be a coach, therapist, close friend, or colleague. Sharing it will help to lighten the load of carrying around the fear of being found out. Fear only thrives when the lights are off. Sharing it with safe people turns the lights on. You may also find that others have similar fears too, and you'll see that you're not alone.

You Don't Need All the Answers

One of the most common fears I see in my clients is the fear of not having the answers. To an impostor, feeling like you don't know everything can lead to feeling like you're a fraud. Take some time to consider how ridiculous this is. One of my biggest fears was not knowing what I'm doing because, unless I had all the answers, I felt like I was a con artist. For me, it led to over-preparing and having under-confidence in myself. It's worth asking whether it's even possible to have all the answers. We see experts go on podcasts and seemingly have an answer for everything, but they don't, because it's just not possible. If it was, why would they continue to research, learn, and practice? Wouldn't they know it all, already?

When the goal is to have all the answers, it takes us back to having a fixed mindset where we're trying to prove our worth instead of improving our skills and learning. I think there's immense confidence and genuine humility (not false humility) in saying, 'I don't have the answer to that.' It shows you're human and, many times, opens up a useful discussion or chance to learn. When you're OK with not knowing all the answers, you no longer have to fear that happening. I will, however, offer you a technique I learned from entrepreneur Grant Cardone that helps soften the blow if you're in an important meeting or giving a presentation and you get asked a question you don't know the answer to. Simply reply with, 'That's a great question. Let me take some time to reflect on this and get back to you.'

You don't have to be an expert at everything and know everything. Jordan Peterson is someone considered an expert and intellectual in the field of psychology and philosophy, yet he says he changes his mind about something every time he gives a lecture.

The person who has all the answers is the person who has stopped learning.

One of the things many clients say is that they want to have the certainty and confidence of their peers, yet nobody has all the answers; they, like you, are still figuring it out. You don't have to be an expert at everything; you just have to keep starting.

LENS CHECK

Take a moment to reflect on what life's like for someone who knows their value and capabilities and owns it. How do they feel about themselves? They are humble and enjoy learning new skills and taking chances to grow and succeed. They don't compare themselves to others but instead track their own progress and efforts as a measure of their success. How do they see new opportunities? They perceive themselves as a master at what they do despite not having all the answers. What does life look like to them?

Impostor syndrome will keep you waiting to feel ready, but now you have a tool kit for breaking these feelings down, it's time to acknowledge your worth and get into action. Impostor feelings and doubt can lead to procrastination, which we'll tackle next.

KEY TAKEAWAYS

- **Impostor syndrome comes from feeling like you know less than you do and that others know more than they do, mixed with the belief of not being good enough.**
- **Share your knowledge and successes with others and remind yourself that people don't know what you know. Doing this not only improves your confidence but increases your opportunities for success.**
- **Let go of needing all the answers. Learn by taking action and updating your perspective, knowledge, and skills.**

CHAPTER 6

Eliminate Procrastination

Everyone procrastinates – it's part of human nature – but that doesn't mean it needs to hold you back or stop you from starting before you're ready. With the right tools, you can learn why you procrastinate, how to catch it faster, and access the switch that turns off procrastination anytime you choose.

One of the major causes of procrastination is perfectionism, but now that you have the tools and mindset to start badly from Chapter 1, that will no longer get in your way. However, there's a deeper root cause of procrastination that we need to uncover, address, and uproot for you to be truly free to take massive action.

Think back to the last time you procrastinated. What were you putting off doing and why? Maybe you were studying for an exam, preparing for a project, wanting to post on social media, writing a book, or planning to make an important phone call, but the moment you thought of doing it, something else became more appealing. In that moment, you might have felt like you couldn't be bothered, or that it was too much hassle. Maybe you blamed yourself for having no willpower. You may have felt overwhelmed by the task or like it was too much for you to take on, or maybe you felt like you couldn't cope with it. You might even have thought you were just being lazy. So many people tell me they're lazy, but I don't buy it. I don't think anyone in their right mind wants to be lazy. Laziness is an excuse, a cover-up for fear and disconnection – it's the surface symptom of a deeper issue.

The problem with procrastination is that there are an infinite number of ways you can do it. You might scroll social media, watch YouTube, tidy the house, or do another task that's less urgent. When you think about it, there are a million other tasks you could be doing other than the one you need to, so why do they become so important when it's time to do the work you need to do? It all comes down to stress.

The Root Cause of Procrastination

Stress is your body's reaction to the perception of threat. The key word I want to highlight in that last sentence is *perception*. It's not the situation itself that's a threat; it's your perception of it that creates the feeling of stress. A change in focus, meaning, and strategy can instantly change the way you see or approach a situation, dissolving your stress and getting you back into action. If you experience a lot of procrastination, it's time for a new approach to handling stress.

When you don't feel ready, you're feeling stress or tension on some level in the body. When you experience stress in the body, it can cause you to go into fight, flight, or freeze mode and, often, our default reaction is to get away from the uncomfortable thoughts and feelings. Reaction stands for 're-action': We re-enact a behavior from the past that we learned to help us survive or cope. As a result, procrastination steps in as an automatic coping mechanism to the perceived threat, showing up as everything from overwhelm and fear of failure to fear of expending energy.

Imagine you have an exam coming up and, when you think about it, you feel stress in the body, which you then try to explain with the thought, 'I feel overwhelmed because of the exam.' You then put off studying and instead watch YouTube. Procrastination persists when you don't eliminate the cause of the stress and you keep having the same reaction every time you experience that feeling. As a result, you continue to cope with the feeling of stress by watching YouTube, putting off the work, doing other tasks, or worrying about it, instead of studying.

LENS CHECK

Take a moment to reflect on what life's like for a master procrastinator. How much action do they take? What do they do with their time? They put off tasks rather than completing them and instead do what feels easy in the moment. How do they feel? How much energy do they have? What's it like for them to miss out on the sense of achievement that comes with completing tasks?

The Procrastination Cycle

We each have a default response to stress. Take a look at the points below. What's your default response?

- Fight: You get defensive, over-prepare, or become irritable.
- Flight: You avoid doing the task, distract yourself, or leave it until the very last minute.
- Freeze: You have an inability to focus, experience anxiety, sit at the desk, and do nothing.

You might experience one response or a combination of all three, depending on the situation. So, why do we experience these stress responses? The prefrontal cortex - the part of the brain responsible for thinking, planning, and rational processing - acts slower than the amygdala, the emotional part of the brain responsible for detecting threats. When the amygdala senses a threat, either real or perceived, it sends an alarm signal to other parts of the brain. It alerts the hypothalamus, which acts as the control center for the autonomic nervous system, activating the body's stress response (fight, flight, or freeze). This signals the adrenal glands to release the stress hormones cortisol and adrenaline. This process can happen very fast. This is why you get hijacked and go offline, often creating the procrastination cycle:

- Trigger (situation that prompts stress)
- Default response (fight/flight/freeze)
- Procrastination (you put off the task)
- Temporary relief

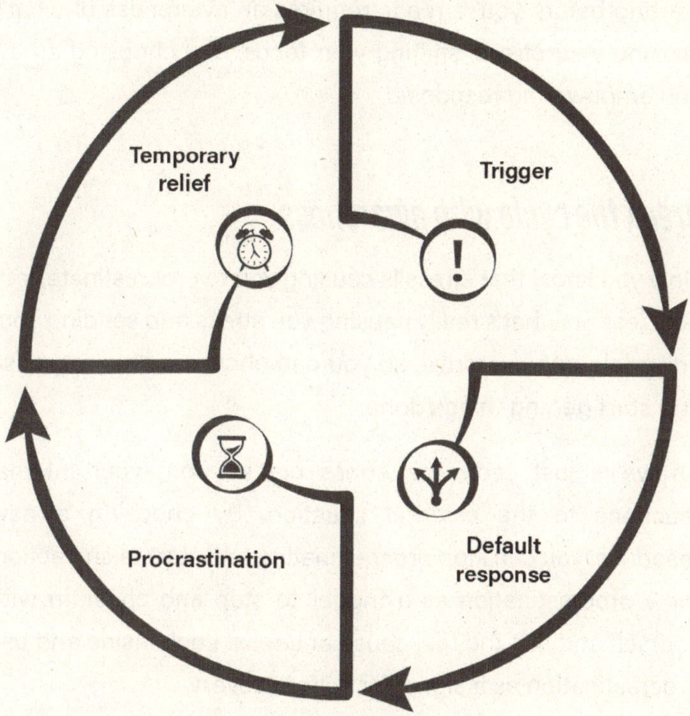

Figure 2: The Procrastination Cycle

While immediate threats do exist, like a tiger in front of you or a car heading toward you at high speed, most threats in the modern world are perceived and aren't a danger to us, and therefore don't warrant such a response. The amygdala helps to transmit emotional memories from stressful events. Therefore, most of the stress we experience is memories and perceptions from the past being reignited and re-enacted in the present. So, we're reacting to a perception in our body and not a real threat. This is much like having a smoke alarm: It's helpful when there's a fire, but the smallest detection of smoke can set it off. The key to breaking free from this cycle and starting before you're ready requires an awareness of what's causing your stress, shifting your focus, and choosing a new and empowering response.

Break the cycle with awareness

Now you know that stress is causing you to procrastinate, let's get clear on what's really causing you stress and sending your amygdala into overdrive, so you can choose a new response and start getting things done.

As we've just seen, the stress comes from your internal reactions to the external situation. By choosing a new response, you can stop procrastinating and start taking action. View procrastination as a trigger to stop and check in with yourself and see the real cause of stress. Look inside and use procrastination as a signal for self-discovery.

The moment you feel stress and want to put off starting, pause and check in with yourself - it isn't the situation creating the stress; it's how you react to it. Putting it off keeps the same unhelpful reactions at play. Pausing and choosing a new response will free you of stress and get you into action.

Trigger + default response = stress

Trigger + new response = inspired action

You can break the procrastination cycle by knowing that it's not the situations that create the stress and the procrastination we experience; it's a lack of awareness about what's causing the stress in the first place that keeps the cycle in play. For example, let's say you have a work deadline coming up and you've set aside two hours to complete the project. When it's time to get started, you find yourself putting off the work and instead reaching for your phone to scroll social media. This is your default response. Before you go down that rabbit hole, you can stop the pattern in its tracks. Breaking the response requires you to stop and ask yourself the following three questions:

1. What emotions am I feeling? *Some stress and worry.*
2. What am I thinking that is causing me to feel this way? *It's all too much and I don't think I'm going to get it done in time.*
3. What do I do to get away from the feeling? *Grab my phone and binge Instagram.*

What I want you to see here is that the stress is coming from the reaction, not the deadline itself. The thought, 'It's all too much and I don't think I'm going to get it done in time' is what creates the feeling of stress. The feelings accompany the perception of threat, and the action is a reaction to the thought and feelings. The more clearly you see the perception of threat versus a real threat, the more free you become and the less stress you experience. You can choose a new response and shift from stress to a solution. At the start, it's helpful to do this exercise on paper, but, with practice, you'll be able to do it on the spot with ease.

This is why your triggers are your biggest teachers. They're teaching you how to understand your stress and release it.

Offer yourself understanding instead of judgment in these situations and you'll break the cycle of procrastination for good:

- Trigger (situation that prompts stress)
- Bring awareness to it and choose a new response
- Take inspired action
- Make progress

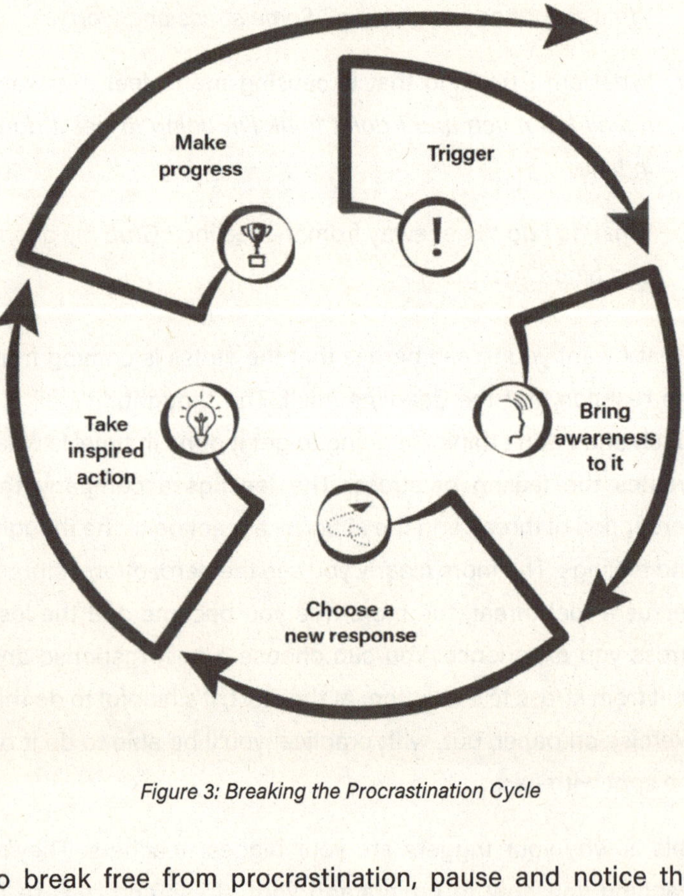

Figure 3: Breaking the Procrastination Cycle

To break free from procrastination, pause and notice the reaction you're having about it and see it as just that – a reaction, not a reality. The more real the reaction seems, the more stress you'll experience and procrastination will continue as you stay stuck in the cycle.

When starting, you'll face the unknown, which can trigger the stress response in you by bringing up the fear of failure or judgment, a lack of control, or overwhelm as the path ahead of you may seem unclear or vague. As the brain struggles to see the steps or have a plan, you may find yourself putting off the tasks and procrastinating as an automatic habit. Pause and ask yourself:

- What's the triggering situation?
- What am I thinking that's creating stress?
- What do I do when I think that thought?
- What new thought or action will help me handle the situation better?

For example:

- What's the triggering situation? *Posting on social media.*
- What am I thinking that's creating stress? *People might judge me or think I look silly.*
- What do I do when I think that thought? *Do other tasks and overthink it.*
- What new thought or action will help me handle the situation better? *Others may judge me but I know I can handle it; their words can't hurt me without my permission. Focus on my purpose, make a video, and post it before I'm ready.*

When you see your reactions, thoughts, and perceptions clearly, you'll be able to shift them so they're no longer able to stop you, and you reclaim your power. You break the cycle with awareness, understanding, and new actions.

EXERCISE

Pause now and ask yourself, 'What am I putting off right now?' Then ask, 'What am I thinking about the task that is causing me to put it off?' This will help you to see the block is in your thinking and not in the task, and you'll be one step closer to taking action.

Anytime you go to put something off, your trigger is teaching you where you can grow, and a new thought or strategy will transform stress into success. When we respond rather than react to stress, it can be something that helps us grow. Just like in the gym when you put your muscles under stress and tension by lifting weights, the muscles learn to grow stronger to adapt next time. Stress isn't a bad thing – it's how you use it that matters. When you're choosing your responses, you'll grow your action muscles.

Procrastination is a habit, but you can break the cycle and therefore break the habit. Below are several other tools you can use in tandem with this new awareness to become an inspired action-taker.

Reduce Demands and Increase Resources

A major cause of stress is when your demands outweigh your resources. Stress arises when either your internal or external demands feel overwhelming or unmanageable. At this point, it can be easy to shut down or run away, but consider that a shift in the number of tasks can change how you feel. Internal demands are the 'musts,' 'shoulds,' and 'have-tos' we looked at in Chapter 1. When demands are higher than resources, your feelings of stress increase; when demands are lower than resources, your feelings of stress decrease. Removing these internal demands and letting go of the expectation of perfection will go a long way to removing the unnecessary stress you experience. Do you expect perfection? Do you expect to succeed first time? Do you expect to never make mistakes? Look at your own expectations and notice whether they're realistic or not. Lower the bar for what you expect of yourself. This will reduce the stress of internal demands and increase your motivation to act.

External demands include the number of tasks you're expected to do, other people's expectations of you, and deadlines. If you have 10 tasks to do in a day and only enough time to complete three of them, that will cause you stress. If my daughter is suddenly off sick from school and I have a full day of coaching calls lined up and need to look after her, that will create stress. It's like trying to fit 10 people into a car that has five seats. The most important thing to see here is that these are problems that can be solved.

With demands, the stress comes from having more tasks than time and thinking there's nothing you can do about it, but there is. Stress only persists by keeping the demands above the resources. It goes when your resources exceed the demands. Here are two solutions to this problem:

1. **Reduce the demands.** Set out to complete three tasks in the day instead of 10. Cancel your calls and look after your daughter, or ask to move a deadline if it's really not manageable. Think about the demands you have in your life now. What demands can you remove or reduce?

2. **Increase your resources.** Delegate some of the tasks to other people or hire someone to help. Call a friend, relative, or babysitter to look after your daughter. What resources do you have? What additional resources or people could help you?

Knowing that you can reduce the demands and increase your resources means you have a way to respond to the situation and get out of stress and into action. Use your creativity to find solutions or look to others who have already solved the challenges you're facing for some ideas.

The planning fallacy

A hidden factor that increases demands is the planning fallacy – a cognitive bias where we underestimate the time, effort, and resources needed to complete a task. You may think that you can get a report done in an hour when it might take a few days; you might think you can get 10 tasks completed in a day when three is plenty; or you might expect to be in peak shape in six weeks when, in reality, it would take six months of hard work in the gym to reach your goal.

Recently, I prepared for a 15-minute speech. I thought I could do it in an afternoon; I was wrong. It took a day to write, a day to memorize, and a day to practice. Luckily, I prepared ahead of time so I didn't have to panic the day before. You might be able to think of times when you expected more of yourself than was possible. Where do you demand a lot from yourself? Where do you overestimate what you can do in the amount of time you have?

The planning fallacy can be a big cause of stress and procrastination as you try to take on too much too soon, making the tasks you want to start feel like mountains to climb. Remember that you're human – even if you're hardworking, you still only have a certain amount of time and energy each day. Ask yourself, 'How much time do I need?' Then give yourself more time than you think you need and you'll find it more manageable, less stressful, and more fun. And, more importantly, you'll actually be able to get started and enjoy being in action

Start Small

Another feature of procrastination is trying to do it all at once, which comes from the black-and-white thinking we explored in Chapter 1. Our brain only has a limited working memory capacity, so when you look at the big picture all at once it causes stress due to cognitive overload, overwhelm, and uncertainty – which then triggers the stress response and, as a result, the procrastination cycle we looked at earlier.

When you're faced with the overwhelm and fear rooted in procrastination, try breaking down the task into steps and taking them one at a time. If they still feel too much, break them down even further. If you think, *I can take it one step at a time and get it done*, the task will start to look more manageable, and the stress and worry will lift.

Another strategy for addressing cognitive overload is to use the two-minute rule to get into action. If you can complete the task in two minutes or less, do it now – make the call, send the email, put the thing away. Speed is a useful tool in starting before you're ready and building a habit of action. You can also use this rule to set a timer and start on your task for two minutes and, after the time is up, stop. This can trick your brain into taking action and you may find that, once you get started, you're enjoying it and want to keep going – if that's the case, go for it!

The two-task trick

Here's a great hack that I discovered works wonders for getting into action and getting things done. Take two tasks that you'd like to complete or make progress on. Then give yourself the choice between the two. The key to this hack lies in you giving your brain the choice. Instead of just asking, 'What should I do?,' which leads your brain to pick the easier task out of all possible options – like watch YouTube, stay in bed, or clean the house – by giving it two specific options, your brain gets a win: It gets a choice but you trick it into doing a task that might still be easier, but actually benefits you. Give it a try – you'll be surprised at how effective this strategy is.

The Cost of Procrastinating

I used to be the king of procrastination. It was so normal for me that it became a way of life. I spent a great deal of time learning about personal development, and it was only when I applied the strategies I learned that I went from procrastinator to action-taker. The tipping point for me was to see the cost of procrastinating. As tasks mounted up, I would feel more stressed, anxious, and overwhelmed. The things I'd been putting off didn't change; problems stayed the same or got worse.

The thing about procrastination is that we put off the task for fear of failing or trying to avoid stress, but putting it off increases stress in the long term and actually speeds up many of the things we don't want. Maybe you don't want to start your business because you fear you might fail so you put it off, but what's the cost? You fail by not starting. If you have debt and procrastinate on paying it off, the cost is that it gains interest and gets bigger. You put off planning your week and then spend the rest of the week chasing your tail and overwhelmed by choice. When you apply the strategies in this book and start before you're ready, you can start your business, or pay off the debt, or set your intentions and wish you had done it sooner.

Putting off tasks doesn't make them go away; rather the costs of not doing them mount up.

They are simply something you have to do, and when the task is completed, you don't have to think about it anymore.

EXERCISE

Take something you're procrastinating on now and write down all the costs of putting it off. What are the costs of not starting the project or going to the gym or doing the thing you need to do? What are the costs of not changing? What are the costs of things still being the same a year from now? Doing this exercise will help you see that short-term inaction creates long-term pain, and short-term action creates long-term success and fulfillment.

Shift Your Focus

One of the big causes of stress that drives wanting to put tasks off is focusing on the parts of the task you don't want, like failing, being judged, or putting in the work. How do you feel when you think about these? Stressed, so no wonder you want to put them off! On the other hand, what does it feel like when you think about the task you want to do as already being completed, and you consider all the benefits? Maybe that's the emails cleared from your inbox, reaching financial freedom, passing the exam, your accounts being done, getting five-star reviews of your new podcast, people loving your product, or your business succeeding and making a positive impact on others. It feels great.

One of my mentors, author of *As The Pendulum Swings* Lindsay Brady, taught me that when you look at what you don't want, you'll feel stressed, but when you think about the desired end result having already been accomplished, and all the benefits of achieving this, you feel good. When you perceive the end result as already true now in your mind, your brain seeks to achieve this. By default, our brain wants to move toward pleasure and away from pain. What happens when you feel good? You're relaxed, motivated, confident, and enthusiastic about taking action. Your brain will want to move toward pleasure and away from pain to achieve that result.

Create an end-result image of how you want things to go: Think about the task you want to start or the thing you're procrastinating on and imagine you've already completed it and it went exactly how you wanted. What benefits does that give you? How would that make you feel? When you have a picture of this in your mind, it sends a positive message to your brain, motivating you into action. When you perceive the results as being true now, you'll trick your brain into getting into action to make this a reality. You'll feel great when the task is finished, so why not tap into this feeling now? Anytime you start to procrastinate, bring the image of the end result you want into your mind and sit with it. This will shift your focus and inspire you into action. When you then accompany this with tiny steps, as we discussed earlier in this chapter, you have a powerful inner tool to remove stress and get you into action.

Setting deadlines is also a great way to force yourself into action, and we'll explore this in Chapter 10.

Practice Mindfulness

Starting before you're ready requires you to step out of your stress-based thoughts for a moment and return to the now, where there is calm and clarity – and mindfulness is the master tool for this.

Mindfulness allows you to observe your thoughts and feelings and not be run by them. Imagine a fight breaking out in a prison and you being in the middle of it – it can be hard to know who started the fight while you're caught up in all the chaos. If you were to step out and go up a few floors of the building and look down at the fight, you could gain some perspective on it. You might see who started it and what's happening, but, most importantly, you'd no longer be involved in it. This is the kind of inner clarity you can gain by being mindful of your thoughts and feelings and returning your awareness to the present moment. The thoughts and feelings are still there, but you can step out of them.

Developer and founder of mindfulness-based stress reduction (MBSR), Jon Kabat-Zinn, describes mindfulness as, 'The awareness that arises from paying attention, on purpose, in the present moment and non-judgmentally.' When you sit and notice the thoughts and feelings you experience without judgment, you create more opportunities to be less reactive and more creative. Sitting and observing the breath for a short period of time will take you out of the reactive thoughts and feelings, and give you space to choose your response.

A study published in *Social Cognitive and Affective Neuroscience* found that participants undergoing an eight-week MBSR program experienced reductions in perceived stress.[2] Meditation and mindfulness can train the brain to be more responsive and

---

2 Hölzel, B.K., et al. (2010), 'Stress reduction correlates with structural changes in the amygdala,' *Social Cognitive and Affective Neuroscience*, 5(1): 11–17.

less reactive, shrinking the amygdala - which, as we've seen, is responsible for reacting - and increasing the prefrontal cortex, the part of the brain responsible for planning, thinking, and organizing projects.

Use mindfulness to bring awareness to your reactions without judgment. You do this by bringing your attention to the sensations in your body - you can notice the feeling of your feet on the floor, your body in the chair, and your breath. When you feel stressed or stuck, space is a powerful way to settle the mind, regain your composure, and put things in perspective. Mindfulness is awareness in the moment and meditation is a great tool to tap into mindfulness and re-center yourself.

The biggest mistake I see people make when new to meditation and mindfulness is expecting to have no thoughts at all - don't do that. The goal is to observe the thoughts without judgment and return your focus to the breath. I've meditated for over 10 years and often my mind will race with thoughts. The goal is to bring awareness to the thoughts, not to have no thoughts at all. As you bring your attention to one focal point, such as the breath, you won't be lost in distraction. This is an invaluable tool for directing your mind on to one task and getting yourself into action.

EXERCISE

The following simple guided meditation is all you need to get going with mindfulness. Start with five minutes and, when you get comfortable with that, move up to 10 minutes. The intention of the meditation is to focus on

the breath, notice when you get distracted in thought, and return to the breath. This will firstly reduce the impact the stressful thoughts have on you and secondly train your focus so you have more control over your mind.

- Find a comfortable position where you won't be disturbed. You can be seated or lying down on the floor. Set a timer for five minutes, close your eyes, and relax.
- Bring your attention to the breath; pay attention to its rise and fall. Notice whether your breathing is deep or shallow, fast or slow.
- Observe and notice any thoughts and judgments that come up. You might notice things like, 'I can't do this' or 'It's all too much,' but watch from an observer perspective.
- Emotions may also arise. Notice them as passing sensations rather than a fixed identity – so 'I feel stress' rather than 'I am stressed.' Seeing thoughts and feelings as temporary and optional gives them less of a hold over you.
- Keep returning your awareness to the breath.
- When the time is up or when you're ready, open your eyes and notice how you feel – maybe you feel lighter or more relaxed, like a weight has been lifted.
- As you return to the present moment, set an intention for your next actions, such as 'I can do this,' 'I am present,' or 'Be here now,' to remind you to stay in the moment and on task.

When you feel busy and stressed, taking time for space is the last thing you want to do, yet it's often the most impactful thing you can do. Meditation is really simple; it's free and it will be the most valuable tool you'll have in your tool kit when it comes to personal growth. Space allows room for you to settle, compose yourself, and get back to your best. When coming out of a meditation, I often feel like I've gone from seeing the world in regular definition to high definition; everything seems brighter and clearer. Mindfulness will also reconnect you with your inner wisdom and intuition that exists beyond your thoughts.

Instead of putting off the task, scrolling, or trying to fix the stress, take a mindful moment, breathe, focus on your body, and notice the sensations without judgment. Allow yourself to relax and take a tiny action toward starting that project, going to the gym, cooking a new meal, facing a fear, or doing whatever it is you want to get done. Start with five minutes of meditation a day and build up to 10 minutes a day – it will have a profound effect on your mindset, focus, and ability to take action.

The more awareness you have of your internal reactions, the less real the threat appears, and the quicker the stress will dissolve, freeing you to step into action.

LENS CHECK

Take a moment to reflect on what life's like for someone who can get into action anytime they choose. They're aware of their stress triggers and how to respond rather

> than react so they can take inspired action. How much do they accomplish? What have they achieved and what kind of success do they create? They enjoy getting things done and focus on how good it feels to complete the task rather than getting bogged down in the aspects they don't enjoy. How focused are they and how much more free time do they have?

As you break out of the procrastination cycle, you'll find yourself building self-trust and self-confidence with every step you take. You're now one step farther on the path to mastering the art of starting before you're ready.

Once you get into action, you'll have to meet and confront the gatekeeper to your freedom, which is fear. Next, we're going to explore how to change the way you experience fear, so it becomes something to move toward instead of something to run from.

KEY TAKEAWAYS

- **See procrastination as a chance to learn about yourself and your triggers. As you choose new responses, you can condition yourself to move from stopping to starting.**
- **Reduce the unnecessary demands and expectations you place on yourself so you experience less stress and more enjoyment while you get things done.**
- **Use meditation as your guide to return to a place of inner calm, presence, and focus, ready for action again.**

CHAPTER 7

Face Your Fears

The moment you have a great idea and go to take action on it, do you feel fear kicking in? Do you fear the judgment of others? Do you fear making mistakes or not knowing what to do? Do you fear getting it wrong? Maybe you're afraid of something bad happening.

Feeling fear is like your foot hitting the brake. Of course, the brakes on a car are useful to keep you safe, but problems arise when your foot stays on the brake when you want to accelerate. Fear can seem like a giant stop sign, but it's not – as we'll explore in this chapter, it's just a caution sign, and there are steps you can take to overcome it.

Stepping into the unknown can bring all your fears up to the surface. Fear can show itself in many ways and it's not always obvious – it has many different disguises. Our fears can show up as our excuses, complaints, justifications, repeated patterns, and frustrations. Maybe you want to start a new hobby, but you 'don't have enough time.' Perhaps you want to leave your relationship or start a new one, but 'it's better to wait until another day,' or maybe you want to set up your business, but you 'don't have the resources or money to.' These are all subtle ways in which fear pulls the strings in our lives. These might all look like real problems, but the problems are created by our fears.

Fear is the uncomfortable feeling you experience when you perceive something might be dangerous. If you have a deep desire to be an action-taker, but feel held back by fear, it's possible you've developed a fear of future fears. 'Anticipatory anxiety' is the fear and apprehension you experience while waiting for something to happen. The longer you wait, the more time there is for anxiety to build up as you sit there thinking about what might go wrong and the bad things that might happen. This keeps you going around in circles, as we discovered in Chapter 4.

Although they may appear the same, fear and anxiety are two different things. Fear is the emotion we experience when facing a present-moment threat and anxiety is a nervous feeling that comes from your assumptions about what might happen in the future. Fear is a present-moment thing and anxiety is a future-based thing. Anxiety is the feeling you experience while avoiding a situation or emotion. Instead of feeling guilt, shame, embarrassment, disappointment, or fear, you spend your time thinking, planning, or avoiding, and hoping it will go away.

One of the biggest causes of anxiety is being anxious about being anxious. I've worked with many people who have experienced this, and often panic attacks are caused by this fear. The thought of having a panic attack causes the attack – the fear of looking silly or being out of control in front of others creates a constriction of energy, and it leads to the very thing you don't want to happen.

Avoiding fear or situations that trigger fear might seem like a good option: After all, why would you want to experience discomfort? But, as I learned the hard way, trying to escape from situations you fear is exactly what keeps the fear alive inside you. As we've seen, what we resist persists. When attempting to avoid fear, you live in your head, which can lead to overthinking, insecurity, and doubt. You might worry about an upcoming presentation or meeting, or maybe you worry about losing money, or you freeze when facing situations you're unsure about. Anxiety gets heightened when you try to control what you can't control. Running away from fear is the reason I lived with anxiety for so many years and wasn't taking action, and it's the same for many of the clients I work with as they wait to feel ready. Fear doesn't go away and you shouldn't want it to – that would be like wanting a car without brakes.

LENS CHECK

Take a moment to reflect on what life's like for someone who experiences chronic fear. How do they feel? They are held back by fear and afraid of experiencing it, so run from anything that might be unknown or scary. What does the future feel like for them? What's it like for them to take action? They focus on what could go wrong and what they don't want to happen. How does the world look to them?

New situations and the unknown require you to experience and tolerate a certain level of uncertainty, because to thrive in life you have to deal with people and circumstances you can't control. As a result, you can't escape feeling fear and uncertainty, but you can change your relationship with it. Starting before you're ready is a lifetime practice, one where you develop the awareness to experience the discomfort of fear and not feeling ready yet, but you commit to take action despite this.

While I offer you tools to help you handle fear and anxiety in this chapter, the first place to start is to meet it, greet it, and accept it. One client I worked with had a fear of panic attacks in public, so it stopped him going out. I asked him, 'What would be the worst thing that would happen?' and he replied, 'Feeling extremely uncomfortable and looking silly in front of others.' I asked, 'Can you be OK with this? Can you choose this?' He did, despite his discomfort, and found that, when no longer resisting the anxiety and fear, it no longer controlled him. Interestingly, research has shown that people who are out there taking action typically experience less anxiety than those who sit around planning, thinking, waiting, and avoiding.[3]

Anxiety is a cage, and being willing to experience fear and move through it is the key to unlocking it.

---

3 Coutinho, M., et al. (2019), 'Experiential avoidance, committed action and quality of life: Differences between college students with and without chronic illness,' *Journal of Health Psychology*, 26(7): 1035–1045; Titov, N., et al. (2024), 'A pilot study examining whether restricting and resuming specific actions systematically changes symptoms of depression and anxiety. A series of N-of-1 trials,' *Behaviour Research and Therapy*, 177.

Think of the journey of self-mastery as becoming a ballroom dancer – life is the dance and your partner is fear. Self-sabotage is sitting on the sidelines and watching everyone else dance, while reading the guide on how to dance, wishing you could do it perfectly. You might be safe on the sidelines, but you don't get to enjoy the dance. It's time to start dancing.

How Fear Holds Us Back

I was standing at the end of a pier in Dorset looking out at the blue ocean, feeling excited about the possibility of running and jumping into the water. I took a deep breath and ran toward the end of the pier, ready to jump in, but, as I got a couple of meters away, something strange happened – my body jolted to a complete and sudden stop. Just a few moments earlier, I couldn't wait to jump into the water, but, as I reached the edge, my body froze and I had no control over it at all. I found this both puzzling and rather amusing. What had just happened? I wanted to jump, I was ready, but I didn't. I walked back up the pier, re-centered myself and made the commitment. This time, I told myself, *I'm going to jump, no matter what my body says.* I sprinted as fast as I could and, again, I felt the resistance and the uncomfortable feelings in my stomach, but I committed to jumping off, and I did. It felt like a breakthrough.

The question I was left to reflect on was: 'Where else in my life am I doing this? Where else am I wanting to act and holding myself back?' Take some time to reflect on this now. Where would you love to jump in, yet you're holding yourself back because of fear? In your career, your relationships, your decisions, areas of adventure and fun in your life, where are you freezing because of fear and what do you fear the most? The pier example is an obvious metaphor for how fear stops us – it causes us to freeze when we're fully capable of taking action. The reason it made me laugh was because I didn't think I was afraid, but I was. I had to stop and admit this to myself before I could finally take the leap. Pretending you're not afraid can keep fear alive as it runs in the background. Acknowledging it, being OK with yourself while you feel it, and taking action regardless is where courage comes into play.

Fear can take over quickly and without awareness – it will have you stuck in a career or relationship that doesn't serve you; it will keep you from being the person you want to be; and it will stop you from sharing your ideas with others that could lead to opportunities for you and them. It doesn't matter who you are or how successful you are, you can't escape fear if you want to grow mentally, emotionally, and spiritually.

If you run from fear, it will chase you, but if you dance with it, you'll transform it.

How you respond to fear will determine the quality of your life, impact the opportunities you either take or miss, and determine whether life is something you have to get through or something you enjoy. It's all in how you hold fear and what kind of relationship you have with it. As New Age writer Stuart Wilde said, 'Your spiritual journey is actually a measure of how much fear you can go beyond.'

Stop Trying to Control What You Can't

One of the major causes of anxiety is trying to control what you can't. When you try desperately to control the outcome, how do you feel? When you try to get other people's approval, how does it make you feel? When you try to get others to understand you or agree with you, how does it make you feel? When you try to control the future or change the past, how does it make you feel?

There are many things in life we can't control and trying to do so leads not only to frustration, but to feeling out of control. Imagine being in a fast rapid that's carrying you downstream. You fear where the rapid might take you, so you desperately try to swim upstream. You waste energy fighting the current and you don't go anywhere as the rapid is too strong. It takes courage to let go and flow with the current. You have to accept you don't know where it will take you and this will feel uncomfortable. It will feel like you're giving up some control, but the reality is you're giving up trying to control what you can't, which is the water. The moment you let go, you gain control, and you're free. You can't control the rapid, but you can steer yourself left and right and go with the flow of the water, rather than against it.

It might seem like a good idea to try to control the future, but have you ever noticed how much difference worry makes? You may try to seek certainty, predictability, and security; however, the future is often unpredictable and unknown, and there are many elements you can't know yet and can't control. In the present, you can plan for the future and prepare for what's ahead and feel a sense of control; you can make decisions now and think about what you need. In the now, you have influence, control, and power. The following exercise will help you to understand what you *can* control so you can experience the freedom of letting go of what you can't.

EXERCISE

Take an area of your life where you want more freedom and power: Maybe it's your relationship, your career, your health, or your finances. Grab your journal and draw a line down the middle of a blank page. On the top left, write 'What I CAN control' and on the top right, write 'What I CAN'T control.'

List everything you can control in the left-hand column and everything you can't control in the right-hand column. Think about things that frustrate you, maybe things you blame or complain about or wish were different, and place them in the correct column. I've included some prompts below to get you started.

What you can control:

- **What you choose to think**
- **The meaning you assign to yourself, others, and situations**
- **What you do and don't do**
- **What you say or don't say**
- **How you use your energy in the present**
- **Your responses to your automatic thoughts and emotions**

- **Your boundaries, patience, discipline, commitment, attitude**
- **The job you're in, skills you learn, your habits**

What you can't control:

- **Other people and their reactions**
- **Your automatic thoughts**
- **Your emotions**
- **Who your parents are**
- **The weather**
- **Your childhood**
- **The past, the future**
- **Your genetics**

Next, circle all the things you can control but are currently not taking action on. For example, setting a schedule, planning your food, setting boundaries, or quitting a job you don't like. Then circle all the things you can't control but are trying to control, even if you're trying to control them in your mind or wish they were different – for example, other people's reactions or the past.

What can you learn from this exercise? Are there any surprises? You can do this exercise anytime you feel anxious or powerless and it will put things back into perspective and help you to decide on what and where you should channel your energy and attention.

When you accept and let go of what you can't control, take responsibility for what you can control, and have the self-awareness to choose, you become fearless.

Surrender

Surrender is choosing to fully accept what you can't control. People often hear the word 'surrender' and think it's about being passive or giving up; however, it's the exact opposite. In fact, it's one of the most powerful tools you can practice. When I played poker, control was something I struggled with the most. I blamed bad luck for my bad runs and often tried to control the outcome of a hand, which distracted me from playing my A game and kept me in fear. When I learned to surrender, I was not only able to play better, but I also felt the anxiety lift as I could enjoy not having to try to control everything. I chose to give up complaining about other players and blaming bad luck or a lack of talent for my losses and I started to focus on making the best decisions I could and let go of what I couldn't control.

Surrender involves trust. You can't surrender while you're holding on. It's not a passive process but an active one. Choose to control what you can and give up any attachment to the outcome. You have to be willing to feel all your emotions for this to be successful. This looks like selling a service and letting go of whether someone will buy it; telling someone you love them and letting go of needing to hear them say it back; sharing an idea in a meeting without needing to control if others will agree with it; or setting up a business because you feel called to without controlling its immediate success.

Just like flowing downstream on the rapid, it takes an extreme amount of courage to say, 'I can't control how this will play out.' To apply this, go back to Chapter 1 (*pages 19–20*) and pick an exercise where you could fail on purpose, look silly, or take a tiny risk and, this time, go for it and play full out. Surrender the outcome, let go fully, and see what difference it makes to how you feel.

Embrace the Fear

Trying to avoid your fears or eliminate them can lead to an unhealthy obsession with personal development, where you keep searching for another book, tool, or technique to make fear go away. It can lead to using personal development as an attempt to escape your feelings and always feel good. The tools are used as an escape route rather than a path to growth. I was in this trap for years until I took the leap from consumer to action-taker. If you're spending 80 percent of your time reading and learning new techniques and not taking action, then fear is at play. When this flips to 20 percent reading and learning and 80 percent taking action, your entire world will shift.

It's OK to be nervous; it's OK to feel fear. These are signs that you're stepping outside your comfort zone and expanding. Every new venture I've been on has been accompanied by fear. If you wait for fear to go away before taking action, you won't take any and will limit yourself. As we've seen throughout the book so far, waiting to feel good all the time and be without fear or discomfort is a trap.

Back in 2017, I had the idea to post a video on Instagram. I had experienced profound shifts in my life, and I wanted to share the lessons I'd learned with the world – or with my 250 followers at that time. My goal was to have a positive impact on just one person. As the inspiration hit me to share, I was met with a barrage of terrifying thoughts: *What if people laugh at me? What if I look like an idiot? What if no one likes it?* I noticed the fearful thoughts coming up, but instead of listening to them, I put my foot on the accelerator, picked up my phone, and pressed the 'record' button. I was ready to face my fears head on; I knew that the only way to be free of them was to surrender to them. I hadn't even done my hair that day and I thought to myself, even better – as a recovering perfectionist, that was simply another fear to face.

I recorded a video and spoke from the heart, with no idea what I'd say; I just knew I had to do it. I talked about my intention to share the life lessons and tools that had helped me overcome anxiety, build confidence, and find deep states of inner peace. To my joy, after posting it, I didn't die, nobody hated me, and in fact people seemed to resonate with it. It had 260 views and a few positive comments. Looking back, I was at my most vulnerable and also my most courageous, and I love that version of me – the version of me that made my purpose more important than my fears. I love the version of me that's willing to be embarrassed, to follow his dreams, and to take risks and step into the unknown.

To overcome my fear of being seen, I created a commitment to post a video and a quote every single day for a year without fail. I came up against the same fears and thoughts most days, and I heard them and acted anyway. Even now, I'll go to post a video and sometimes the little voice in my head will say, 'It's not good enough' or 'What if people don't like it?' but I post it anyway. I surrender myself to starting before I'm ready.

Five years later, in July 2022, an idea popped into my head for a video: the three mistakes that kill our confidence. I took out my phone, filmed it, and shared it online. This time the video got 2.3 million views, 90,000 likes, and 29,000 people saved it to watch back. It had over 600 comments, with many people saying thank you, because it was just what they needed to hear. There were a few haters, but that's social media for you. Making videos for me now is easy and enjoyable because I've made thousands. Don't expect to be great straight away: As we learned when we looked at the four levels of competence in Chapter 5 (*see page 103*), you have to do something many times to get great at it, and for the fear to fade away. This is why it helps to follow your passions and do the things you love.

You overcome your fears by making the unknown known and by putting your foot on the accelerator, catching when your foot wants to go on the brake and making the conscious choice to return to the accelerator again and again. Be thankful you have a brake, but be even more thankful you have an accelerator – that's what's needed to take you where you want to go. The accelerator is what gives life to your higher self.

EXERCISE

If you've been held back by fear, it's time to break free and show yourself that you're no longer willing to stay trapped in its cage.

Ask yourself now:

- **What's something I'd love to do but have been held back by fear?**
- **Why is it important for me to overcome this fear?**
- **What can I commit to do every day to face it?**

Here's a rule I created that transformed my relationship with fear: If it scares me and I want to do it, then I'm going to do it. This is starting before you're ready in motion. So, what does this look like in practice? Do you want to leave your Christmas party, but don't want to look rude? Take action and leave. Do you want to film your first video and put it online, but you're scared? Film it and post it. Do you want to say sorry to your friend for a past mistake, but you're worried you'll come off looking weak? Call them, say sorry, and own it. Do you want to tell the person who has pushed in front of you in the queue that you were next, but you're scared they might get cross? Take a deep breath and let them know.

It doesn't have to be the biggest, craziest thing; fear is personal to each of us. We all have different perceptions and different fears. Speaking on stage may be easy for some people, but saying 'no' to their boss terrifies them. Climbing a tall building is child's play for some, but cooking a new meal for a friend makes them anxious. There's no courage without fear.

Remember that the result is less important than the freedom you gain by doing something you didn't think you could.

Shift Your Perceptions

The greatest freedom you can have in life is the freedom to think what you want to think. Probably the biggest insight I ever had about fear that changed everything for me was that fear cannot exist outside of me. It exists in my thoughts and judgments about the world around me. Your feelings are a real experience, but the thoughts that create them are not. You can choose fearful thoughts or fun thoughts. While you can't control the thoughts that pop into your head, you can choose what you do with them.

EXERCISE

Take a moment somewhere you can relax and not be disturbed. When you're ready, I want you to think about something you're really afraid of – something you really wouldn't want to do or have happen, something around a seven out of 10 on the discomfort scale. Have you got it? It could be speaking on stage, your boss shouting at you, going broke, doing a bungee jump, or being at the top of a tall building looking down.

Give yourself a moment to think about the thing you're afraid of – really picture yourself being there, doing it, and experiencing it. Imagine what you see and feel the emotions that come with it. What do you notice? What do you experience in your body? Does your heart rate go up? Do your palms start to sweat? Does your mind race? Notice your bodily reactions to the *thoughts* you're having about this fearful situation, which you aren't actually in.

This simple thought exercise goes to prove something significant: You're not afraid of the situation itself, because you're not there and it's not happening right now. It's only happening in your head. You're instead afraid of the thought of it happening. We scare ourselves with our scary thoughts.

Fear exists in your *perception* about the upcoming situation. The perception is a message to your brain about the possible danger, but it's not the danger itself. Getting on a plane can turn into 'The plane is going to go down in flames with me on it.' The message determines how you feel, not the situation, and the message isn't real – it's an interpretation of the situation.

This is why fear and procrastination are often so interwoven, as you learned earlier. People aren't lazy, they're afraid. Buddhist monk Thich Nhat Hanh said, 'The fear, the anger, and the despair is born on the ground of wrong perception.'

Fear cannot exist without the thinking that's happening inside your head. Now here's the secret:

The thoughts that hold the power are the thoughts you give power to.

Read that again, because this understanding can change your life. When we give power to the thought 'People will judge me,' we breathe life into it and it becomes more real. If we breathe life into the thought 'People will respect me,' this will become real instead.

Get to know the unknown

Think about something you were once afraid of but now enjoy or can do. Maybe you feared a new job and felt terrified on the first day as you didn't know the role or the people, but, once you settled in, you grew to love the work and the people there. Has there been a business or hobby you feared you might fail at or mess up only to learn, grow, and thrive? Even exercise can feel scary and overwhelming in the beginning as it's painful, exhausting, and uncomfortable. You may fear the discomfort and then, over time, enjoy the progress and health benefits, and find the pump you get when lifting weights or the endorphin rush you get after a run exhilarating. How about traveling? I remember the first time I set foot in Thailand and went to Khaosan Road in Bangkok – I felt terrified of the noise, how hectic it felt, the cars and bikes, and the drastically different culture from what I was used to, but within 24 hours, I felt relaxed, had met the local people, spoken with other tourists, enjoyed the food, and I was excited to be there. If I had run away, I would've missed out on the adventure.

Everything new starts out as unknown. New can feel scary, but as you get to know it, your perception of it changes from unknown and scary to known and safe, and, dare I say it, even enjoyable. Remind yourself of this as you take steps and the brakes go on and the uncomfortable feelings arise. It's not the place that's scary, it's that you don't know it yet. The more you get to know the thing you're afraid of, the less afraid of it you'll be.

If you fear judgment, it's likely you avoid it like the plague. If you fear embarrassment, then you'll be shy and reserved to avoid experiencing it. If you fear starting new tasks and failing, you'll avoid doing so and become more afraid of it. However, as you lean in and take the steps, you learn and understand more. With a new job, you may learn about the company, get to know the employees and the skills of the role. With a new relationship, you can get to know the other person and share things about yourself, a little bit at a time. We judge what we don't know, but when we understand situations or people fully, they appear different, less fearful. Give yourself time to get to know the thing you're afraid of and you'll transform it. As you speak on stage, it becomes less scary and more exciting. As you move to a new home and get to know the area, you may discover places you fall in love with.

Find Freedom from Fear

If fear exists in your thoughts and not in the situation itself, this means that the more time you spend in your head thinking about the situation you don't want, the more fearful you'll be. This is what fuels the anticipatory anxiety we met earlier.

Although, as we saw in Chapter 4, you can change your thoughts, this isn't 100 percent necessary in order to let go of fear and take action. Instead, you can spend more time in the present moment - which is your direct experience of the now without the distortion of thought. When you become aware of your thoughts but not lost in them, you're present, and when you're fully present, there's no fear because, as we've seen, fear is a thought, not a reality.

Being fearless doesn't mean having no fear at all; it means having less fear, and the more time you spend noticing when you're lost in fearful thinking and return to the present, the less fearful you'll be and the more effective you'll become. Being present doesn't require you to do anything - you simply need to 'be.' When you allow your thoughts to settle and quieten the mind, you are free. No judgment, fear, anxiety, or worry can exist without a thought. When your mind is still, you see life from pure perception, untainted by the veil of thought.

One thing you can do to aid your return to the present moment is to use the breath, consciously taking longer inhales and exhaling fully. Exhaling activates the parasympathetic nervous system, which promotes relaxation and rest. When you exhale, your vagus nerve is stimulated, leading to a decrease in heart rate as the relaxation response is activated. The vagus nerve is one of the most important nerves in the body. It originates in the brain stem and extends down through the neck and into your chest and abdomen, reaching the heart, lungs, and gut. By slowing down your breath, you can trick yourself into relaxing and, as a result, actually relax. When you're relaxed, you're less stimulated by and lost in thought, and it's here where you have more access to being, rather than thinking and doing.

EXERCISE

My favorite breathwork technique is box breathing:

- **Take a breath in and count to four.**
- **Hold your breath for a count of four.**
- **Exhale for a count of four.**
- **Pause for a count of four.**

Repeat this four times or as many times as needed until you feel calm. As you breathe in deeply, feel your belly expand, and exhale slowly, letting your belly soften.

Just knowing I can use my breathing to get present has been a game changer for me. I hope it helps you too.

Stop Making Excuses

As we saw at the start of the chapter, fear can be hidden in your excuses. Your excuses are what you see on the surface, but they aren't the truth and are often a mask for a deeper fear underneath. The thought of 'I don't know what I'm doing' is an excuse and underneath it is the real fear that 'If I try and fail people might judge me for it.' 'I don't have enough time' is another excuse. It's so sneaky because it seems so true if you have a busy schedule, but it's often a mask for something deeper – perhaps the fear of having to say 'no' to others and set boundaries, the fear of having to let others down if you cancel plans, the fear of asking for support and bothering others, or the fear of delegating tasks to others. It could even be a combination of many fears working together.

It's easier to make an excuse or to complain than to take action and do something about it. Real problems do exist – maybe you don't have a lot of spare time to work on your business, maybe you do feel stressed, maybe you don't know what you're doing – but these only stay as problems if you keep the excuses alive that support them and don't explore the deeper fears hiding underneath. When you own your excuses, take responsibility for them, and commit to solving them, you can take actions to transform them. The bonus is you get to dismantle your fears in the process and feel freer.

What am I afraid of? What do I believe? Is it true? If it's a 'no' then let's go!

When you call out your excuses, you confront your fears head on, and the beautiful thing is you'll see the truth – like we saw in Chapter 1, as Alan Watts said, your fears are merely ghosts. I've had so many conversations with clients that resulted in 'aha' moments, when they saw that, hidden underneath their excuses, was the truth that they were afraid of not being good enough. The only way out is to tell yourself the truth and take action. To live free from fear you must live in the knowing that your excuses are a mask for your fears, and they only exist in your mind; they're not real. When you give up your excuses, you stop fear from controlling your life. On the other side of your fear is your true self waiting to greet you. The only limit you have is a thought. It's time to get clarity on your fears and the excuses covering them up.

EXERCISE

The key with this exercise is to see that your excuses cover up your beliefs and your beliefs aren't true. By revealing them and owning them, you can be free of them!

1. **Name a goal or something you want to do but are afraid of.**
2. **Name the excuse around why you haven't started yet.**
3. **Name the fear underneath the excuse: What are you really afraid of?**
4. **Name the belief that is creating the fear.**
5. **Ask yourself, 'Is it true? Is it a fact or a belief?'**
6. **Take one tiny step toward your goal.**
7. **Trust the process.**

You can repeat this exercise as many times as necessary. It's important to do this on paper to begin with so your brain doesn't trick you, but over time, you'll find that you can do this on the spot and quickly move into action.

Act Upon Your Insights

We discussed connecting to your intuition when it comes to making decisions in Chapter 2, but it also plays a part in overcoming fear. When you get an insight or an inspired idea, it's a message from a higher part of you – it comes from the inside and pops into your head. This could be a person to call, a great business idea, or the solution to a problem you have. These are the inspired ideas from your intuition and inner wisdom. They are new, surprising, and often unexplained ideas – things to get excited about and act upon. However, how many times have you had an amazing idea only for fear to shut it down? Perhaps you had the idea to email your boss about a new business opportunity and then the fear arrived: 'What if they think it's stupid? What if they put it into action and it leads to something bad? What if I can't pull it off?' or maybe even more subtle than that – 'It's the weekend, I won't bother them now' – and the idea and the enthusiasm around it fades. This can cause the brakes to go on, you put the idea away for another time, and it goes into the vault of great ideas you never act on.

Moving from insight into action is where you get to live in alignment with your true self and disprove many of your fears. The book you'd love to write, the relationship you want to start, the gym you want to join, or the person you want to message – it's never too late; your ideas are inspired because they come from a higher part of you. The faster you can act on them, the faster you can stop fearful thinking from stopping you – just as you saw me do in Chapter 4, when I acted from my heart, not my head, and asked my wife's dad for permission to marry her. You can use any of the tools in this book to help you get into action and out of fear. When you act on your insights, one of two things will happen:

1. The thing you're afraid of doesn't happen.

2. You get an outcome you didn't want, but you handle it and survive.

As Susan Jeffers reveals in her best-selling book *Feel the Fear and Do It Anyway*, the fear under all our fears is that we won't be able to handle it. When you know that you can handle anything, you have nothing to be afraid of. And the truth is you've handled everything you've experienced up until this point today, so you can.

As you get to know your inner self, you'll feel less like you don't know what you're doing because you'll trust yourself to step into the unknown and be OK with what happens. Not only do you trust yourself, but your reason for doing what you're doing becomes more powerful than your fears. There's something at play that's far greater than doubt and judgment. You can accept your fears, trust your inner guidance, and develop a powerful ability to respond to whatever life throws your way. The more you get to know yourself, the less afraid you'll be. The more you get to know the new task, new job, or new person, the less afraid you'll be.

LENS CHECK

Take a moment to reflect on what life's like for someone who is fearless – they feel fear but use it as a sign to act. How do they feel about themselves? They know in their heart that fear is a result of their thinking, and with a shift in perspective and action they can dance with fear. How do the world and other people look to them? They feel fear as excitement and energy to use as fuel for their spiritual growth. How much action do they take?

Each time you move away from a situation that creates fear, you reinforce the fear and teach your brain that you're afraid of fear. When you move toward fear, you teach yourself that you're someone courageous. It's a muscle you flex and the more you flex it, the stronger it gets. Don't expect fear to go away. Instead, learn to choose the unknown, trust yourself, surrender to all possibilities, and keep starting before you're ready.

Next, we're going to tackle one of the biggest barriers that holds people back from their true potential, power, and freedom to take authentic action: caring what other people think.

KEY TAKEAWAYS

- **Fear is a caution sign, not a stop sign. Remember, fear exists in your perception of a situation, not the situation itself. So lean into your fears by taking action when you want to, even when it's uncomfortable.**
- **Focus on what you can control and let go of what you can't. Surrender to the unknown by letting go fully and living in the now.**
- **Your fears hide in your excuses. Call out your excuses, see them clearly, and then take action to break free from them.**

CHAPTER 8

Stop Caring What People Think of You

I was lying on the floor of the London Underground, at the busy interchange at Bank station between the Northern line and Central line, while people walked all around me. My heart was pounding and I was terrified about what people were going to think of me for lying on the floor of a station for no good reason. Would the people walking by laugh at me or humiliate me? Would they throw stuff at me? Would the police come and tell me off or arrest me? I took deep breaths and tried to calm myself down, reminding myself that I was safe and that the only person's approval I needed was my own.

It was my body that needed to learn this – my heart kept beating as if I was about to be attacked, but I was teaching it that I could handle it through my actions. As I relaxed, I looked around and noticed that no one was paying much attention to me. A kind old lady asked me if I was OK, to which I smiled and nodded.

There I was, lying on the floor and the people walking past me were too focused on themselves and the concerns they had about their day to care. After 30 seconds, I jumped up feeling proud of myself. I had done something strange in public to embarrass myself on purpose and nothing bad had happened. I felt liberated.

When you care what other people think of you, it restricts you from taking action with freedom and enjoyment, and it makes life feel very... serious. Everything can be a chance to be criticized and judged, to feel embarrassment and shame. Perhaps you want to start a new hobby but worry about looking silly in front of others. Or maybe you want to express yourself but feel you might offend others. Do you want to set up a business, but don't want to fail and look foolish? All these fears are based in how much you care about other people's opinions of you. Worrying what others think of you can also manifest itself as people-pleasing and wanting to be liked, to fit in and not rock the boat. It's steeped in a deep desire to belong and be accepted.

I spent years worrying what others think: It stopped me from sharing my opinion and, in fact, even having an opinion in the first place, for fear of others disliking it or them not liking me because of it. I would water myself down to the point where there was no me left to share. I didn't know what to wear or what to say and was often very shy. As it did for me, overcoming these fears and worries will change everything for you; it will give you your life back.

LENS CHECK

Take a moment to reflect on what life's like for someone who is crippled by the fear of what others think about them. How do they feel about being judged? They worry about how they're perceived by those around them, and project these worries out onto others. How do they view other people? How do they feel about themselves? How free are they? What's life like when they need others to approve of everything they do?

In the last chapter, we looked at how facing your fears can set you free, but what I've discovered for myself, and seen in almost every client I've ever worked with, is that our deepest fears involve how we relate to others. Now we'll take transforming fear one step further and explore why you care about what others think, and how to stop caring and instead focus on what truly matters to you. Not caring what other people think of you is spiritual enlightenment. It's the freedom to be yourself totally and enjoy life on your terms, without the prison of other people's opinions keeping you stuck.

Where People-Pleasing Comes From

It can be incredibly helpful to know the real reason why you and I care so much about what people think of us: Where does this come from and why is it such a problem for so many of us? As human beings, we all desire connection – it's a survival instinct, where a sense of acceptance and belonging can make us feel safe. From the moment we're born, we're helpless. In the first few years of life, we're totally dependent on our parents or caregivers to hold us, feed us, care for us, clothe us, and teach us how to navigate the world.

The adults hold all the power and children depend on adults to get their emotional, psychological, and safety needs met. Children don't need to cook their own meals, go to work, or pay the bills – these are all taken care of by the adults. The children rely on the adults to survive. If the parent doesn't look after the child and doesn't meet their needs, the child can feel a terrifying sense of abandonment. So, as children, many of us learned to seek approval as a way of getting our needs met. Parents and caregivers make many decisions for children, including what and when they eat or how much TV they watch. This can create a dynamic of 'If you do what I want then you'll get what you want' and 'If you don't do what I want then you won't get what you want.' This want goes deeper – it is a *need* for love and acceptance.

The disapproving looks and actions of parents can feel immensely unsafe for a child and, for many children, they learn to abandon their own needs and authentic expression to get their needs met and gain acceptance from their parents. When your needs aren't met in childhood, which include being listened to, having your feelings acknowledged, and feeling accepted, you can form the belief that you're not worthy as you are, creating internalized feelings of shame. You therefore only feel worthy when meeting the needs, expectations, and demands of others – and this is when the seeds are planted for behaviors like people-pleasing, perfectionism, and avoidance. If, as an adult, you still have the belief that you *need* others' approval and acceptance, disapproval will feel unsafe and you'll be living as an adult with a childhood map. This results in waiting for others to make decisions for you, not wanting to disagree with other people, and needing to be liked to feel safe. This is part of why you don't feel ready to start - you're waiting until you know you'll succeed and won't be judged by others.

EXERCISE

It can be helpful to explore who you seek approval from and where this shows up for you in your life to understand the impact it has on your personal freedom and ability to get into action. Ask yourself:

- **Whose approval do I seek the most? Write down a list - it's not uncommon to seek it from everyone.**
- **What are the ways I seek approval?**
- **What are the ways I avoid judgment or disapproval?**

Doing this inner discovery work will show you areas where you're restricted by the opinions of others and point toward where you can have a breakthrough if you're willing to stop seeking approval from others and, instead, start approving of yourself.

One of the key mindset shifts you can make to stop caring what others think about you is to see that the needs from childhood turn into demands as an adult. It's your own demand that others should approve of *you* that creates the problem. This shows up on a subconscious level as 'Other people must like me.' When you see that it's *you* demanding approval from others, you can consciously choose to let this demand go – you can free yourself of the need for approval and no longer care what people think of you.

By making the decision today that 'Other people can disapprove of me if they want,' you no longer have to go around demanding approval from others. This means that you don't need people to agree with you, you don't need to be liked, and you can allow others to have their opinions without having to change them. You can let go and be free – what a weight off your shoulders. When you make this mindset shift, you'll notice you feel more relaxed and others will pick up on your energy and feel more relaxed around you – when you don't demand approval from them, you allow them to be themselves too.

As an adult, you don't *need* others' approval to be safe. You can want it, but you don't need it. However, your belief system needs to catch up with this. Your body may still react as if there's a threat to your well-being, even just at the thought of others judging you. However, this comes from a faulty belief and a reaction to your feelings. If someone disapproves of you, it might feel uncomfortable, but it doesn't need to be terrifying. If your boss fires you, you could still get another job. If your partner left you, it would be upsetting, but you could find another partner or find happiness on your own. Thinking you need that 'one' thing keeps you in scarcity and fear. Most people avoid this possibility by either caretaking for others or falling into the routine of being taken care of, known as co-dependency.

When you learn to be comfortable on your own, meet your own needs, and enjoy your own company, you'll be in a place of independence. It's here that you can move to a place of interdependence by learning to partner with others without relying on them to meet your needs. This can be in relationships, friendships, and in business. This is what coaching is: two people working together to create new results. My clients often get the best results when they don't need coaching but they want it. You can support someone without them relying on you to give them what they need, and vice versa.

I first stumbled across the core belief that causes us to worry what others think while reading *No More Mr. Nice Guy* by Dr. Robert Glover. In the book, he describes the life script that many of us take on in childhood that keeps us stuck: 'If you're "good" and do everything "right" you will be loved, get your needs met, and have a problem-free life.' The result of this script is to hide our flaws, be who we think others want us to be, and avoid making mistakes or looking foolish in front of others. When this map doesn't take us where we want to go, guess what we do? Try even harder and do more of the same thing that doesn't work. When the people-pleaser isn't liked, they double down and try to please more. It's like a fly trying to get out of a closed window – they keep flying into it because they're not aware that the glass is preventing their freedom. This is what it's like to wait until you're ready. If only the fly could see the glass, then they could find an alternative route to break free.

Shift this childhood script to: 'You are OK as you are and worthy of being loved and having your needs met.' Start living into this and you can teach yourself that you don't need others' approval to be safe. Empowerment and authenticity is available to you right now when you shift this childhood script and start before you're ready, proving to yourself that you can be safe and thrive as an adult.

As you take on new challenges and step out of your comfort zone, you might face criticism, rejection, failure, and judgment. The faulty beliefs you acquired in childhood place your focus on the outside, meaning you look outward for others' opinions as a way to make your decisions and live your life. It's time to embrace the disapproval of other people and put the focus back where it belongs: on the inside so you can start living your life with purpose, passion, and freedom.

Focus on What *You* Care About

What you focus on determines where your energy goes, because where attention goes energy flows. When your attention is on what people think about you, it's not on what matters most to you; instead, it's on survival strategies and self-protection. Maybe you have a presentation to give at work or a project to prepare for and your mind starts to drift toward, 'What if the team doesn't like it?' or 'What if it's not good enough?' All the focus is on worrying what other people think about *you* rather than on the value you can offer them. This creates a self-consciousness where you start to question and critique yourself rather than focusing on what really matters and the purpose of the project. It becomes about how you look rather than what's important and how you can serve others.

Focusing on what people think of you will take you away from the purpose you worked so hard to identify in Chapter 3. Breaking free requires a shift in your focus from what others think about you to what you want to do and why.

The reason why you do something is more important than what others think about it.

Your life can be about how you look or about what's important to you. Dr. Wayne Dyer calls this 'appearances versus quality thinking.' Why do you go to the gym? Is it to look good for others or to feel good about yourself and your health? Why do you want to buy a new car? Is it because you want others to think you look cool in it or because you love nice cars and want to ride in luxury? Why are you giving a presentation? Is it to impress the team with how good you are or to add value to the team?

Of course, you might buy the car and find that no one really cares about it or maybe you get a few nice comments and people then forget. You might spend hours working out in the gym and eat only salad in preparation for a date and not connect with the other person emotionally. You might give the presentation and impress everyone, but they don't learn anything from what you shared. You can't control what other people think, do, or want, and so doing things for their approval is a gamble – you're gambling with your time, effort, and self-worth. When you shift from 'What do they want me to do?' to 'What do I want to do and why?' you take back control.

Take the project, task, or action you want to start and ask yourself, 'What's the outcome I want to achieve? Why is that important to me? What steps do I need to take to reach the outcome I want?' These questions will help you to focus on the purpose and meaning behind what you want to do and bring your attention to the process, instead of what people will think, which takes you away from what really matters to you. These are also the elements you can control versus other people's opinions, which you can't.

Another tool to shift your perspective is to move from 'What will others think of it?' to 'Do I love it?' When you fall in love with the process, what you do, and why you do it, you'll find the focus gets taken off your 'self' and you'll lose yourself in the flow of what you're doing.

Shift from Self-Conscious to Self-Aware

'The spotlight effect' is a cognitive bias where people overestimate how much others are paying attention to them. They may feel people are looking at their appearance or actions and maybe even criticizing or judging them. This can lead to a heightened sense of self-consciousness and anxiety in social situations, and focusing on your personal flaws or differences. When you walk into a restaurant, it might feel like the whole room stops to look at you, or when you give a speech and fumble some words, you assume everyone noticed it and will remember it forever. When you're self-conscious, you're focused on yourself and worry about the tiny details and how others perceive you.

An antidote to this is to become self-aware. When you notice the thoughts you have about yourself without judgment, they'll no longer have power over you. Self-consciousness is judgmental and self-awareness is non-judgmental, as you take a more objective view of the situation and yourself. Self-consciousness is like looking at your reflection in the mirror and worrying about how you look, criticizing what you see, and being anxious about what others think of you. It's an external spotlight.

Self-awareness is an internal spotlight – it's like turning a light on inside, with the aim of better understanding yourself. Self-consciousness is worrying what people think about you and thinking, *Am I talking too much? Do they like me? Do I look awkward?* It's thinking you shouldn't be feeling how you are, just like, as a child, you may not have been allowed to be awkward or stand out or be yourself. Self-awareness is thinking, *I'm feeling a little awkward and I don't know what to say*, and then thinking, *That's OK, I'll start a conversation*. You're tuned into your thoughts, without them being a problem.

When you're self-conscious, the judgment determines how you feel and it restricts you. It's like seeing there's only one option on the menu: anxiety. When you're self-aware, other options open up to you, like understanding, compassion, and even excitement. From this space, you also see that what others think about you is coming from your thinking in the moment, not from them. When you're not wrestling with your own thoughts, you'll see people are much friendlier than you had imagined.

We all judge each other – it's self-protection – but when you bring love and kindness to others, you open the door to connection. As we touched on in Chapter 1, life is like a mirror: When you judge others as mean, you'll see mean people everywhere. The opposite is true, too. I once had a client show up for a session who seemed completely uninterested. I asked what they wanted to work on and they had nothing to share and made no effort. It would have been easy to judge them as not coachable, or focus on myself and think I wasn't wanted as a coach, but, instead, I stayed curious. I asked what was on their mind, gave them space, and sought to understand where they were coming from. An hour later and they said the session had been very helpful for them.

Notice any worries you have about what people think of you without 'buying into' them. Notice what judgments you have about others. Observe your need for approval without judging yourself for it. There's a power tool you can bring to both your own and others' judgments, and that's curiosity. If someone says, 'You're selfish,' instead of reacting to it, you could get curious and ask, 'What makes them say that?' or 'What must their view of the world be for them to think that?' You could see that this is how they think, not how it is. The same is true for yourself. If you think, *They'll judge me*, instead of buying it, get curious. What evidence do you have to prove this is true? Can you know they will? Is it possible they won't?

Judgment is an attempt to avoid the unknown and gain control, but it often backfires. Stay curious and open and you'll find that many of the judgments and fears you had start to loosen up a little.

Self-conscious: You feel anxious and wonder what people think about you, and you think that you shouldn't be anxious.

Self-aware: You notice you're experiencing some anxious feelings but recognize that's OK and take deep breaths to calm your mind and body.

Update Your Inner Child

The part of you that still cares what people think of you is your inner child. This part of you still holds the beliefs and emotions you experienced as a child. Situations that trigger your inner child's beliefs can cause this part of you to activate. You might feel like a child if your boss gives you negative feedback or when someone says 'no' to you or tells you what to do.

It's at this point that awareness is key: Where do you feel afraid of others? When do you feel powerless or out of control? Where do you feel like a child in relation to another person? This can often be when facing a boss, an authority figure, a parent, or even a mentor or someone you look up to. Notice when you feel this way and don't react by running away from it. Instead, lean in with self-compassion and understanding.

Your inner child needs to be shown that it's safe to be seen and they need you to give them the permission and guidance now. When you avoid situations where your inner child is activated, you don't teach them that it can be safe and, as a result, the child in you makes the decisions for you. When I lay down on the floor of the Underground station, I was teaching my inner child that it was safe to be seen and that

I can love myself regardless of what people think of me. I felt embarrassment and let it run through me, processing the feelings and shifting my self-perceptions, and transformation took place – I was different afterward. The fears in my mind that had been holding me back my whole life weren't true. I didn't have to let what people think of me dictate how I lived my life anymore. It takes many moments of courage to update your inner child to feel safe, seen, and heard.

EXERCISE

As you step into situations that trigger your inner child, try using the affirmation: 'You are safe, you are OK, you can do it.' Speak the affirmation using the word 'you' because this is your adult self reminding your inner child that you're safe and supported. You're an adult now and you don't need the approval of others to feel safe. This is a very powerful technique because you're affirming these words to yourself to make you feel safe, in the same way I would say to my children, 'You are OK, you are safe' when they need my support. You're being a leader for yourself, from the inside.

If you want to take this process further and do the deep inner work on yourself, you can integrate your adult self with your inner child using the exercise below. With my clients, I facilitate the process and they do this as a dialogue with themselves, sitting and facing their inner child and then swapping roles with their present-day self. You can do the same or make it a journal exercise; both work well. If this exercise brings up strong reactions or even the thought of it is overwhelming, I recommend seeking professional guidance or support with this process.

EXERCISE

First, take the role of your current adult self and answer the following questions:

- **What would you like to say to your inner child?**
- **What do you need them to understand?**
- **What else do you need to tell them?**
- **What do you need from them?**

Next, mentally take on the role of your inner child and talking to your adult self:

- **What do you need them to know?**
- **What do you need them to understand?**
- **What else do you need to tell them?**
- **What do you need from them?**

Continue this as many times as you need to feel fully heard. This process may be challenging at first. If you haven't had time to get to know this part of you, it can feel like you're rebuilding a long-lost relationship.

Next, take on the perspective of a wise observer who has just witnessed this exchange and answer these questions:

- **What did you notice about the exchange?**
- **What advice would you like to give to them both?**

Finally, answer the following questions:

- **How has speaking with those different parts of you changed things?**
- **What was it like? What did you learn about yourself?**

This exercise will help you to integrate your present-day self with your inner child and support you in understanding yourself. It will enable you to bring compassion and awareness to all parts of you, and to meet your own needs when stepping into new roles and projects. While doing this work, you may discover and appreciate hidden aspects of yourself. You may find out that you need more time for play, creativity, and fun. You can be both powerful and childlike at the same time.

As each part of you is heard and given a seat at the table, a new energy can be tapped into and unlocked.

When stepping into new situations, your inner child may often rise up feeling unsafe. You can try to avoid or suppress it, but they're with you whether you like it or not. So, the key is to own them, be proud of them, and work with them. This is why vulnerability is so powerful – to let yourself be seen and be OK with who you are and how you feel. It's a powerful way to integrate all parts of you to be aligned as you take action.

Be Willing to Look Silly

If you were OK with being embarrassed, what would you have to be afraid of? If you were willing to look foolish, what could stop you? How much freedom would this give you? Here's the thing: You decide what you get embarrassed about and what you don't.

My daughter, who is five, and son, who is three, often dance around the house naked – they haven't yet learned that this might be embarrassing. We learn embarrassment through a process called 'emotional mirroring' where we observe how others react to our behavior. As children, we look to others' reactions to make sense of the world around us. If a child drops a toy and it smashes and someone gets angry, they learn that's a bad thing to do. We also learn through modeling – if someone gets caught with the toilet door open and feels embarrassed and blushes, it teaches us to feel the same in similar moments later in life.

You learn what to be embarrassed about by observing others around you. It might be helpful to be embarrassed about walking down the street naked – you could get arrested for it – but it's not so helpful being embarrassed about your less-than-high-quality dance moves when you bust them out on the dance floor. I purposely filmed many of my social media videos in public – on the train and in the middle of busy streets in London – because it was what I wanted to do, and I made the decision not to let the feelings of embarrassment stop me.

If *you* make it OK for you to do the thing you want to do, you can rewire your mental and emotional reactions to embarrassment and stop caring about what others think. You don't react to others' opinions of you, you react to your internal perception of their opinion, and you can change that!

Take a moment now to ask yourself, 'What does the fear of embarrassment hold me back from?' (This could be making social media content, dancing, giving a presentation, or giving someone honest feedback they might not like.) 'What would it be like for me to be free from this?'

Take the thing you want to do but feel embarrassed about and, instead of assuming others are judging you, remind yourself they probably don't care as much as you think – remember the spotlight effect (*see page 178*). Practice making it something *you* choose not to be embarrassed about anymore. Make it OK to make mistakes and feel uncomfortable or have awkward conversations. You have to take action and do the thing; thinking differently is not enough. You need to show yourself that you can do it and feel the emotions in your body as you take bold actions. Through repeated exposure to the new experiences, you'll teach yourself and your inner child that you're free to do what you choose. If you want to walk around your own home naked as an adult, make it OK to do so because you choose to make it so. Don't judge yourself for it. When I lay down on the floor in public, I did it to overcome the fear of judgment and the faulty paradigm that resulted in my overestimating how much people notice me. I had a breakthrough there like no other because I faced the challenge, felt the feelings, and showed myself I could be safe.

The first thing to know is that you're not alone – nearly every person experiences the spotlight effect at some point in their life where they overestimate how much others are paying attention to them. Social media has blown up this bias where, every day, people are putting themselves out into the spotlight. In a study on the spotlight effect in 2000, college students were asked to wear a T-shirt with a picture of Barry Manilow's face on it to class.[4] The T-shirt wearers estimated that 50 percent of people would notice them, yet only 23 percent did. This research highlights how people overestimate how much others notice their actions and appearance.

The fear of the spotlight can show up as worrying what people will think if you quit your job, set up a new social media page or website, start a new hobby, wear new clothes to work, or get a new haircut. When you feel like everyone is looking at you and thinking about you, it will cause you to agonize over your every move. People are too busy focusing on themselves to be thinking about you and, when you truly see this, you are free. As the Stoic philosopher Seneca said, 'We suffer more in imagination than in reality.' Being willing to look silly is a superpower – you choose to be OK looking silly and, as a result, the opinions of others no longer stop you from doing the things you want to do.

It's time to let go and get OK with looking silly in the pursuit of starting before you're ready and living life on your terms.

---

4 Gilovich, T., et al. (2000), 'The Spotlight Effect in Social Judgment: An Egocentric Bias in Estimates of the Salience of One's Own Actions and Appearance,' *Journal of Personality and Social Psychology*, 78(2): 211–222.

EXERCISE

If you've already done one of the exercises in Chapter 1 (*page 20*), then you'll be warmed up and ready to go. Choose from one of the following:

Level 1:

- **Walk along the street in a public place with both arms above your head for 10 seconds for no reason.**
- **Start a conversation with a stranger and see how long you can keep it going for.**
- **Say 'hello' to people as you walk down the street (as a bonus, get high fives – I do this while out running).**

Level 2:

- **Wear a wacky item of clothing to work or to the gym.**
- **Ask for directions to a place you're standing right in front of.**
- **Take an improv comedy class.**
- **Speak at a toastmaster's event.**
- **Walk backward for 10 seconds while in a busy place.**

Level 3:

- **Lie down on the floor in a busy public place for 30 seconds.**
- **Ask for a free coffee in a coffee shop.**
- **Ask for a tour of the kitchen in a restaurant.**
- **Sing a song or do a dance in public while others are around (another one I like to do while out running).**

Remember, the purpose of this exercise is to do it and choose not to be embarrassed or ashamed of yourself. I've done all these exercises myself and, while they're challenging, they're also liberating. Feel the feelings, don't try to stop them, but *choose* what it means and what you think about it.

If someone rejects you or judges you, it means they don't want what you're offering or don't understand; it doesn't mean there's anything wrong with you – there isn't. When people are judging, they're not understanding and, when they're willing to understand, they won't judge you. When you have lain on the floor of an Underground station to overcome your fear of what others think, you'll salute the next person you see doing it.

I recently saw a runner put out their hand to high five me, and I thought, *What a legend!* If you'd never done it before, you might think they're a weirdo – it's all about perspective. This is why curiosity will be one of your greatest gifts in life. The version of me who got up after lying down on the floor for 30 seconds was a new person, one free from the confines of others' opinions.

Feel free to make up your own challenges or tailor them to your own situation or area you want to break through in. When you're willing to look foolish, there'll be no stopping you.

LENS CHECK

Take a moment to reflect on what life's like for someone who doesn't care what people think about them. They live life true to their values and truth and see others' opinions of them as something they can take or leave. How do they feel about themselves? What kind of freedom do they have knowing that the only approval they need is their own? Other people appear supportive and safe to them. How much action do they take? How do they dress and act now that they can be however they want to be?

As you allow yourself to be judged and not take yourself so seriously, you'll feel a lightness about yourself and life. You'll be free to start, be authentic, and try out new things without pressure. In the next chapter, I'm going to offer you the foundation to doing this with inner security as we explore how to build your confidence from the inside.

KEY TAKEAWAYS

- **Be willing to look silly in the pursuit of your own personal freedom and start new challenges without caring what others think of you.**
- **Update your inner child, build a relationship with this part of you, and show them that you can handle anything that comes your way.**
- **Get out of your comfort zone. Change only happens with action, so start today and take on one of the challenges.**

CHAPTER 9

Unlock the Secret to Self-Confidence

I know some of you will have skipped straight to this chapter, looking for quick tips on building confidence and, if this is you, all power to you – it's what I would have done myself. But I've left this as the penultimate chapter because, as I said in Chapter 1, thinking that you need confidence to start is a myth. I hope you've realized by now that when you stop overthinking, procrastinating, worrying about what other people think of you, and start facing your fears, you can get into action, starting now. All the tools you have gathered to this point have chipped away at those blocks that are holding you back and you've already started building self-confidence and experience through courage. This is the last piece of the puzzle and, as you'll come to see, it's the very foundation of starting before you're ready.

First, it's important that you understand exactly what I mean by self-confidence. Self-confidence is not about how much money you have, how much success you've created, or how much other people like you. All of this happens outside of you. If your confidence comes when you have money, you'll be afraid of losing it. If it comes from your success, you'll lose it every time you don't succeed. If it comes from what others think of you, you'll lose it when people dislike you. Looking for confidence in results, validation, or any place outside of you leads to what's called 'swing confidence': When you do well you feel great about yourself and when you fail you feel bad about yourself.

In this chapter, I'm not just going to give you a bunch of steps to give you confidence that will come and go; that would be a disservice. Instead, I'm going to share the true meaning of self-confidence, which goes beyond any tool, technique, or step. If you commit to reading this whole chapter, you won't need anything outside of yourself to feel confident again because you'll realize you have it within yourself.

Signs of Low Confidence

When you have low confidence, you never feel ready and your confidence exists some time off in the future: 'When I have more money, then I'll be confident,' 'When I have more experience, then I'll be confident,' or 'When I succeed, then I'll feel confident.' As a result, you avoid taking on new challenges, hesitate to try new things, and never step out of your comfort zone. You wait to feel confident before taking action and this prevents you from gaining valuable experience and learning new skills. You only take on the tasks you know you'll succeed at and only share your opinion with others when you're 100 percent sure you're correct or that they'll agree. You may find yourself seeking reassurance, checking in with others to see if you're doing it right, or asking them what you should do. You constantly question yourself and your abilities, wondering if your skills are good enough. You might find yourself comparing yourself to others.

You might overly praise people when it's not necessary in an attempt to win their approval, or put yourself down and highlight your flaws as a way of staying small and avoiding rejection. To many people's surprise, the opposite can also be true. Trying to dominate or control others and be right also comes from a lack of self-confidence, where people feel the need to prove they're better than others and display a sense of superiority because they don't believe or feel it for themselves on the inside.

Lacking self-confidence leads to procrastination, avoidance, and a lack of action. Although it might seem like people with high self-confidence are everywhere, they are, in my experience, very rare. Most people who appear loud and confident on the outside are, in fact, overcompensating for low self-worth on the inside. People with true self-confidence are assertive, happy, and self-assured. They have a genuine love for life, for themselves, and others. They don't need to put others down, judge others, or prove themselves – the same way a lion prowls through the jungle knowing its place. These people are few and far between.

Self-confidence isn't something you can hold in your hands – therefore, it isn't a goal, a result, an achievement, or a form of success. It's a good feeling; we're all looking to feel confident because, when you do, you feel good about yourself. Think about what confidence feels like for you: How do you know you have it? If you had all the success, money, and approval you'd want, how would you feel? This feeling is available for you now. There's nothing you need to do to get it – it's who you truly are. When you feel good about yourself and value who you are, you can take on the world.

> ### LENS CHECK
>
> Take a moment to reflect on what life's like for someone who has no self-confidence. They don't back themselves to succeed and wish one day they could be confident. How do they feel about themselves? They look to others for the answers and for permission to take action. How do they relate to others? What does the future look like for them?

The good news is, as we embark on this chapter, I'll reveal how you can build rock-solid confidence from the inside so you can access your innate confidence, feel good about yourself, and be one of the rare people walking the Earth who knows their value and lives from it.

How to Build Self-Confidence

There are two types of confidence. First, there's confidence in what you do – this comes from experience as you build skills and practice them to gain knowledge and competence (the unconscious competence we learned about in Chapter 5 – *see page 105*). We all have confidence in certain areas, such as cooking, sport, driving, or communicating, and we lack confidence in others, such as DIY, meeting new people, or speaking on stage. You don't have to be confident at everything, but you can build confidence in anything if you trust yourself, put in the work, and build unconscious competence.

Confidence in what you do comes *after* you learn the skill. Most people wait to feel confident before they take action. They want to feel confident at networking before they've ever been to a networking event. They want to be confident in their new role before they've even started it. They want to be confident in their business before they launch it. This creates a catch-22 situation where their confidence exists some time off in the future and they never have it!

Being a beginner and moving toward being an expert is on a sliding scale – the journey never ends and, as you grow, you'll need to get used to feeling uncertain, uncomfortable, and having doubts at the start. This is why you need to be willing to look silly, as we saw in the last chapter, and start before you're ready. How can you be confident in DIY if you've never put up a shelf? How can you be confident writing a book when you haven't written one before? How can you be confident in your first business when you've never had one before?

**You don't need confidence before you start;
confidence comes with experience, practice, and time.**

Everyone starts at the bottom and works their way up – this takes humility. While building new skills, you need to be OK with not being great at the beginning and starting before you have confidence in the thing. You have to trust the process.

The second type of confidence is confidence in who you are. This is how you feel about yourself; how much you value, appreciate, and respect yourself; and how much you *trust* yourself to take action and build your abilities. So, how do you get confidence in yourself?

Courage is the secret ingredient

Courage is the bridge between you and the confidence you want, and trust is what it takes to cross the bridge. Courage is your willingness to bet on yourself when you feel fear and to act when you're unsure.

Imagine you're at the top of a tall building. The nearest building is 15 meters away and you've been asked to cross from one building to the other using a long plank of wood that's only 30 centimeters wide with no safety net and you've never done it before. How would you feel about it? It's possible you could make it across, but the fear of falling would be immense. If you fall, it's not going to be good, and would result in serious injury or worse, death. Now, imagine again you're at the top of the same building and you've been asked to cross, only this time there's a large safety net suspended underneath the plank, guaranteeing your safety. How would you feel now? Maybe you'd have some nerves, but there wouldn't be the terror. You might even feel excited about the challenge of getting to the other side.

The gap in between the buildings represents the gap between where you are and where you want to be – between who you are and who you want to be, or the thing you want to start and get great at. It takes courage to start and cross. The lack of a safety net represents a lack of self-confidence. When, each time you try something new, you feel like you might risk it all, you'll wait and avoid crossing, as your fear of failure is so high. The safety net represents having self-confidence - knowing that you can take the steps and fail or fall but get up and go again. This means you can have the courage to cross and try it out - you can back yourself to make it across. The safety net is what gives you the confidence to step into the new and unknown, to start before you're ready, and play full out. It doesn't remove the feelings, but it makes them feel manageable because you trust you'll be OK. What I'll be offering you in the sections that follow is a safety net, which comes in the form of self-love and is built through unconditional self-acceptance, self-trust, and self-responsibility.

Cultivate Unconditional Self-Acceptance

The moment you take on a new role, a new challenge, or a new opportunity, doubt will arise. You've never done it before, so how can you be confident? But, as we've seen, you don't need to be confident in the skills - you don't have them yet; you need confidence in your ability to acquire the skills. You need to back yourself to take the actions and have the belief that you can do it. But how can you do that with self-doubt and self-judgment getting in the way? Most people wait for the doubtful thoughts to clear or try to get rid of them before they take action. But what you resist persists because you push against it and therefore experience more of the thoughts and feelings you don't want. It's like waiting for the rain to stop before going out for a run and staring at the rain hoping it will stop. Instead, take action and just go running in the rain with doubtful thoughts – they don't have to stop you.

When you focus on your doubts too much and try to get rid of them, you attach to the doubts and the judgments, like 'I can't do it' and 'I'm not good enough.' The inner critic that we met in Chapter 4 whispers, 'Don't cross, it's not safe. People will laugh at you if you fall.' And you listen to it and don't take action; you wait to feel ready. The key here is that you can have doubt and critical thoughts and still act. You can have the thought of not being good enough and not buy into it and still value yourself highly – and the master tool to do this is unconditional self-acceptance. This means to love and accept yourself with all thoughts and feelings, without conditions. You are not your thoughts – you are the one who gets to choose them. You are the awareness of your thoughts, a spiritual essence, and this is the key to your confidence.

You are already enough: Your value as a person can never be questioned or changed. As a baby you start out life already enough, then you take on thoughts about yourself and believe that you're not enough, even though it's not true. You spend your whole life trying to prove you are enough. Instead, rest in the feeling that you are. When you return back home, to being enough, and live from here, you'll already have all the confidence you've ever dreamed of.

You are always worthy, just for being here and for being human.

Allow yourself a moment to let this sink in. Absorb this deep into your soul. You may add skills and succeed, but no matter what happens, you are already enough; there is nothing you have to do or prove to have this. Nothing can take your value away from you.

If you knew your worth as a person couldn't change no matter what you do, how would you live? What would you do differently? How free would you feel? This gift is yours; you can claim it right now. It's a decision you make about yourself; it's an awareness you have.

The best way to practice this is to do the comfort zone challenges in Chapters 1 and 8 (*see pages 20 and 188*) grounded in this awareness. Lie down on the floor in public and know you are still enough; leave a typo in an email or risk hearing 'no' and know you are enough – this is true freedom.

The real fear and discomfort underneath not feeling ready yet is believing that you being good enough can change, or that your value as a person can change. They can't. If I made a tear in a £20 note would it lose its value? No. If I stamped on it, would it lose its value? No. If I gave it away to someone else, would it lose its value? No. When you truly know that you are enough and worthy as a person and nothing can change this, you are free. You can start and risk failure without it meaning anything about you. You can do any job you want and earn as much or as little as you want without it meaning anything about you.

You don't need to prove yourself, you don't need to impress anyone, because you already have all the value you need. You can build skills and grow – not because you have to, but because you choose to. From this place, life becomes a game, where you can risk, play, and enjoy yourself. You can be yourself, you can start anything, anytime; you can fail too, because you are always already enough.

The opposite of this - conditional self-acceptance - is only accepting and valuing yourself when you succeed, have positive thoughts, and feel confident, and this is the mistake many people make. The truth is, you can have any thoughts and still be confident because remember, *your thoughts are not who you really are*. They're lying to you.

You are not your thoughts

I used to think I was my thoughts. This created most of my problems and caused the majority of my low self-confidence because I *thought* I wasn't good enough and doubted myself. It was so real that I believed it to be true and didn't think it could change. I thought that new things were scary and I thought that people were just born confident. I believed this for 30 years and so it felt very true. Then it occurred to me that I didn't feel confident because I was thinking I wasn't and, if I started thinking I was, then I could be. Using the tools and insights in this book, I acted on these new thoughts, started taking confident actions, and proved my past doubts wrong.

But it goes much deeper than this: True confidence is what lies beyond your thoughts. There's a wisdom in you waiting to be felt and expressed, and this is where your confidence is. It's a good feeling deep inside of you, before your thoughts. It's your authentic self. One day, years ago, as I sat on the sofa in my flat in London, I fully experienced that I was not my thoughts – I was the feeling underneath them, and this feeling has never left me. Since then, I learned not to identify with my thoughts.

If you are your thoughts, then who are you when you're not thinking? If you stop thinking, do you die? If you are your thoughts, that would mean who you are is constantly changing. In the morning, you might think, *I can't cope*, and so you're an incapable person, and in the afternoon you might think, *I can do it now*, and so you're a capable person. Which one are you? This would also mean you can only be confident when you have confident thoughts, which is why a lot of people experience swing confidence or only act when they're in the right mood or when they're thinking positive thoughts.

Your thoughts change all the time – doubt is normal and so is having doubtful thoughts, but they're not who you are. Your thoughts don't define you and they don't have to control you. You are not your inner critic or your inner doubts, which means you don't have to listen to them.

You have enough critics in life, don't be your own.

Any thought or judgment that blocks you from being confident is not true – it's merely a thought in your mind, and it's optional. When people say they've 'lost their confidence,' the truth is that they've started thinking insecure thoughts. It's your ego talking, not your true self. You might not be able to control the thoughts that pop into your head, but you can choose whether you listen to them. Your thoughts change all the time, and accepting yourself unconditionally is accepting yourself with all thoughts and feelings – and knowing you can change them. It's the deepest form of self-love and a powerful place to live from.

Choose a thought about yourself right now that you want – try it on and own it: 'I am amazing,' 'I am confident,' 'I am capable,' or 'I love myself.' You get to choose what you think, who you are, and what you do.

If you believe all your thoughts to be true, they'll control you, but when you practice not identifying with them, they lose power over you. Imagine you're an actor playing a role in a movie. The character you play might be nervous, insecure, or doubtful, but you know it's just a role you're playing. You don't confuse who you are with the character's fears and doubts because you know who you really are beyond the script. Confidence comes when you stop identifying with the roles you've been playing and start identifying with your true self – the one who is aware, free, and capable. Just like an actor can step out of a role, you can step out of your limiting thoughts and into your most confident self. Identify with the awareness, not with the roles you've been playing. As you get into action, doubtful thinking may arise, but the key is to notice the thoughts and take action anyway. Self-mastery requires you to master the relationship you have with your thoughts.

Say, 'I am having the thought of self-doubt' and then take action, instead of saying, 'I am doubting myself' and allowing it to make you freeze. Say, 'I am having some anxious feelings' and take action, instead of saying, 'I am anxious' and letting it stop you. This will help you begin to separate the real you from your unhelpful thoughts and get you doing what you want, not what your thoughts dictate. This will be essential as you step onto new ground and build self-belief. Don't let the thoughts drive your actions - courage is taking action and betting on yourself, even when you feel fear and have doubtful thoughts.

You are not your actions

Unconditional self-acceptance also means accepting yourself with all actions. This is a tough one for most people, but once achieved, it's life changing. Are you your actions? If you make a mistake, does that mean you are the mistake? If you wrote a book, does that mean you are the book? No, of course not. Yes, you're 100 percent responsible for your actions and their consequences, but you are not them. The same is true for others. Your actions can change over time. You'll make mistakes and then succeed. You might do poorly at a particular skill and then improve. Take someone who has smoked for 20 years. If they quit instantly and never smoke again, are they still a smoker? No, because their actions have changed. They *were* a smoker. If someone who smoked was their actions, then they would cease to exist once they stopped smoking. If your actions are constantly changing, then you can't be them.

Changing what you think and do will change who you become. Thinking you are your actions is what stops people starting or crossing the plank - it makes them scared to do the wrong thing and make a mistake because they identify with their mistakes. Knowing that you are not what you do is your safety net, allowing you to learn and grow.

If you feel like your worth is attached to your career, identity, or actions, you'll be scared to make a wrong move. Everything becomes a chance to sabotage your self-worth and value. When you own your actions but don't identify with them, you're free to take bold and inspired actions, to change them, and trust yourself fully. Start saying, 'I did it wrong' and stop saying, 'I am wrong.' This moves you away from the intense feelings of shame and toward self-love. Say, 'That was a stupid thing to do' and not, 'I am stupid.' Be critical about your actions and kind to yourself. Refuse to judge and blame yourself as a person and, instead, focus on the actions that you want to change, and you'll notice your self-confidence increase at a phenomenal rate!

Replace blame with responsibility

An easy mistake to make is confusing blame with responsibility – one removes your confidence and the other gives it back to you. The number one factor that prevents people from having self-confidence is blaming themselves for their mistakes. This makes their mistakes permanent.

Take any mistake you've ever made. If you say, 'I made a mistake,' you're correct. It's a fact. If you say, 'I made a mistake and that means I'm a bad person,' you're making a very costly thought error. Being a bad person is a moral judgment that leads to blame and shame. Statements such as, 'I am bad,' 'I am wrong as a person,' 'I'm not good enough,' or 'I'm not worthy' are what kill your confidence and cause you to feel like you're crossing the plank without a safety net every time you take action on new ground. To have unshakable confidence is to know, in every cell of your body, that this is a lie.

People don't learn to change through judgment and blame; they learn to hide so they don't get caught next time. But what you hide hurts you, and it's what leads to addictions and unnecessary suffering. Owning your limitations helps you to transcend them. Blame is an attempt to escape responsibility. Learning comes through understanding, where you see new choices that lead to new outcomes. When you remove self-blame and replace it with self-acceptance and understanding, you'll be free to try new things and take calculated risks. Taking responsibility for your actions gives you access to your inner power.

EXERCISE

Pause for a moment and ask yourself these questions:

- **What do I blame myself for the most?**
- **What do I blame others for?**
- **What is this costing me?**
- **What do I need to understand about myself/others? (Remind yourself that you are not your actions and neither are they; you are the one responsible for your actions and others are responsible for theirs.)**
- **What do I need to take responsibility for?**
- **What actions do I need to take in order to take responsibility?**
- **What difference would this make to my life?**

The most powerful tool you'll have in giving up blame and replacing it with responsibility is to practice letting go of needing to be right and making yourself wrong. Blame is all about who's at fault and then being right about it. Maybe you could have taken more time and prevented a mistake, or maybe you or someone else didn't perform a task how you wanted them to, but being right only justifies the blame. It's the cement that keeps it in place, keeping you stuck and powerless. Letting go of being right dismantles blame. Try it out on yourself or others and choose to forgive instead of blame. As you drop out of anger, hate, and resentment, you'll drop into peace, contentment, and self-love.

A mantra that has helped me on this journey is: 'I can get it wrong, but I can never *be* wrong.' Try it for yourself and see how this connects you back with yourself in the present moment. When you stop getting on your back and making yourself wrong, you can give yourself a chance to put things right.

While self-acceptance is the safety net, crossing the plank is building trust, so let's look at that now.

Build Self-Trust

People who lack self-confidence say they'll do things and then don't do them. The cycle of making promises to themselves and others and not keeping them erodes their self-confidence and reinforces their lack of self-trust. But if you don't take action, you can't build the skills, and you won't build self-trust. This is why I've included so many exercises and action steps in this book. When you don't do what you say you'll do, you break trust with yourself.

The word confidence comes from the Latin *con*, which means 'with' and *fidere*, which means 'trust'; therefore, having self-confidence means trusting yourself to keep the promises you make to yourself. When you say you'll go to the gym and you don't, you break trust in yourself. If you say you'll set up your new website by the end of the week and you don't, you give yourself evidence that you don't follow through. When you say to a friend you'll meet them at 5 p.m. and you don't, you're not just breaking your promise to them, you're breaking the promise you made with *yourself* to meet them; it still affects you. Trust is another word for belief and, when you build trust, you build the belief that you can do something. This applies to every skill you take on – the more you practice, the more you build belief – but this also applies to the relationship you have with yourself. When you do the things you say you will, you build trust in yourself and therefore belief in yourself. You become someone you can count on.

If you say you're going to talk to that person and you do, you build confidence. If you say you're going to set up your website by the end of the week and you do, you build confidence. If you say you're going for a run and you do, you build confidence. Each time you act on your inspired ideas, you build trust in your inner self, strengthening your connection to your intuition, integrity, and your internal compass. Own your actions and make yourself accountable for them. Don't make yourself wrong if you mess up; simply own it and go again. Your brain learns from your actions, not from your thoughts.

Honor your promises to yourself, even when you're unsure if you'll succeed or not – this is crossing planks and how you build self-confidence. Former CEO of Coca-Cola, Muhtar Kent, said, 'Success is making a promise into the future without a predetermined outcome.' Success is in the actions, not the result. It's about having the courage to cross, not just getting to the other side. Make promises and keep them by taking action.

EXERCISE

For the next week, make a tiny promise to yourself each day and keep it, regardless of how you feel or what thoughts you have, and watch your self-belief build right before your eyes.

Shift your language

Stop saying, 'I might' and start saying, 'I will.' This will take the doubt out of your promises and help you build inner trust. If someone said, 'I might come into work today,' how confident in them would you be? If they said, 'I'll be there at 9 a.m.,' how would you feel? You create your world with the words you say, and you experience the results with the actions you take.

Seek your own approval

People who lack confidence are constantly checking in with others to see if they're doing it right. Anyone taking on a new job or task needs input, advice, and support from others as they build new skills, but when looking to others for reassurance becomes a way of life, it's a problem. Asking others if your clothes look good or what you should eat for lunch takes away your inner confidence and self-trust, because you think that other people know best, creating the co-dependency we touched on in the last chapter, which undermines your personal authority. If your boss constantly asked you what you thought about their decisions or what they should do, would you trust them to lead you? Getting opinions can be helpful, but constantly needing others to tell you what to do isn't. Seeking validation creates more doubt in yourself, your intuition, and your worth because it doesn't offer you the chance to build self-trust, listen to your inner wisdom, and learn what you like, thus disconnecting you from your authentic self.

Start trusting your own ideas and actions. Notice anytime you want to ask others for something and instead look inside yourself for the answers and decide for yourself. Instead of saying, 'What do you think I should do?' ask yourself, 'What's true for me right now?' This will give you a chance to build trust in your intuition, abilities, and creativity.

EXERCISE

Identify one area where you've been waiting for approval or reassurance and take action without asking. Afterward, reflect: What did you learn by giving yourself permission to act? Of course, use your discernment with this and don't do anything reckless.

Be honest with yourself

This is a game changer in building your confidence. What does it feel like when you lie? You can feel like an impostor – it feels weak and uncertain. How about when you're speaking your truth? You feel certain because you know that what you're saying is true for you. When you're honest with yourself and others, you'll be your most confident, even when it's scary. So speak your truth, talk in facts, and be real.

Human biologist, biohacker, and longevity expert Gary Brecka speaks about a research project called the Spane Scale of Emotion, where researchers put 25,000 people into a room and measured the frequencies leaving their body.[5] They discovered that the most powerful frequency was authenticity, which they found was 4,000 times more powerful than love. Gary describes authenticity as: 'When your words are truthful and you believe what you're saying.' This is powerful because speaking what's true for you comes from a deeper place. It's not just what you've learned or been taught, it's what you know, what you stand for, and what you believe at your core. Your truth is a certainty. It's congruent with who you are; it's power.

How does being authentic apply when you're speaking into the future, when the outcome is unclear? What about having belief in the things you haven't done yet? Many people are afraid to speak with power unless they've done something before, but that's not how confidence is built. You don't need to know how it will go when you're sure you want to take the step. Authenticity is knowing it's the right path for you, not

---

5 Brecka, G. (2024), 'The Frequency of Authenticity' [Video]. Available from: https://www.youtube.com/shorts/BJWjHL4LBHc [Accessed 14 April 2025].

how it will turn out. A belief isn't something that's true – it's not a fact, it's a thought you *choose* to believe, either consciously or unconsciously. So, consider the beliefs you want to be your authentic truth. The beliefs you don't want are a lie. For example, saying you're not good enough is a lie because you don't want it to be true. On the other hand, you may want to believe 'I'm the best in my profession' or 'I'm totally confident.' These beliefs come from inside of you, not from what you learned about yourself. These beliefs may feel less certain initially, if you have never believed them before, but if you *want* to believe them then they are authentic to you.

Your beliefs grow with action. Speak your truth, be honest, and have the courage to speak beliefs you want into the future and act upon them. I created the belief that I am an author and pictured it every day, spoke it out loud, and acted upon it. 'I am an author' was the seed and writing was the water that helped it grow. You're now reading the fruits that tree has grown. I can't control how it will be received, but I was certain that I wanted to write it, and that certainty was all I needed. This can be true for you, too. Choose what you want to believe in, speak it as if it's true, and live into it with action.

Shift your self-perceptions

When you believe you can't do it, you won't, and when you're convinced you can do it, you will. Your beliefs come from your perceptions, and your perceptions are the way you make sense of your thoughts and yourself. Your perceptions of yourself determine your level of confidence and how easy or hard it is for you to start. They inform how you understand yourself and the world. Perception is the thing I'm most passionate about in life because I know that when you change your perceptions, your whole world changes. Your perceptions give you access to self-trust or block it, depending on whether you see yourself as someone who can or someone who can't. If you perceive yourself as someone who can't do something, you'll doubt yourself, hold back, and take no action, not giving yourself a chance to build self-trust.

Each of us creates perceptions about who we are throughout our lives. You're not born with your perceptions; you develop and learn them over time. If a parent leaves, then you might form the perception that you weren't good enough. If you fail an exam, you might perceive yourself as stupid, or maybe someone else said that and you perceived it to be true. If your friends laugh at you, you may perceive yourself as unlovable. These perceptions are often unconscious decisions we make about ourselves and then these become who we 'think we are.' So many of my clients, before they do this work, think they are 'bad,' 'wrong,' 'not smart,' or 'not a confident person.' None of these perceptions are true, but, without awareness, they can feel as true as the ground you walk on and you build a whole identity on top of them. This is why it's important not to believe all your thoughts and to know that who you really are is much greater than that. Your true authentic self is the version of you before you learned to doubt yourself or took on any other perception that limits you in some way.

Your perceptions, often formed without conscious awareness, create the identity you carry with you or the role you play for your whole life. Left unchecked, you can live your life believing these false perceptions and doing yourself a tremendous disservice, until you see that you are not your perceptions themselves and then they become optional – and you become free.

Think about any area of your life where you feel a lack of confidence. How do you perceive yourself in that situation? What perception do you have about yourself? Think back to the earliest times in your life. What situations led to you perceiving yourself that way?

For me, it wasn't just one perception – there were many moments when I created perceptions about myself and others that were limiting and unhelpful. There was the time when I caught two friends of mine talking about me behind my back and I formed the perception that people secretly didn't like me. There was the time when I got punched in the face and didn't fight back in front of the whole school and I perceived myself as weak. There was the time when I smashed a car headlight with a golf ball and I formed the perception that I was a bad person. It was all happening inside my head, in my thoughts, innocently and automatically, without my awareness. I was making these situations mean something about me in a way that would shape how I responded to the world. These false perceptions created my identity, one that limited me. 'I am a bad person' became an identity, 'I am weak' became an identity, and striving for perfection is what came on top of these as a way to hide and make up for them.

The perceptions you have about yourself are filters – they drive your emotions and actions by providing the meanings you attribute to yourself and the world. They determine what you do and don't do, and what ideas and behaviors you accept or reject. Someone could say you look great and, if you have the perception that you're attractive, you'll believe them. If they say you look great and you have the perception that you're unattractive, you won't believe them. Your perceptions stay in your awareness, running your life until you see them for what they are – just that: perceptions; thoughts and meanings you assign to yourself and not facts – and not an identity you have to keep.

When you change the perceptions you have about yourself, you change. If you want to have confidence in yourself to step into the unknown, then you can't bring your limiting self-perceptions with you. They have to go; they are your only limit. You have to see them as thoughts not facts because without them, you are unlimited.

EXERCISE

Grab your journal. Write down all the limiting perceptions you have about yourself and your abilities. Common false perceptions I see in my clients include:

- **'I am not good enough.'**
- **'I am too old.'**
- **'I can't do it.'**
- **'I am bad at starting.'**
- **'I don't like challenges.'**
- **'I don't know what I'm doing.'**
- **'I am not confident.'**

- **'People don't like me.'**
- **'I'll never be confident.'**
- **'I am ugly.'**
- **'I am not smart enough.'**
- **'I am not much fun.'**
- **'I am not good at new things.'**
- **'I am lazy.'**

Perhaps some of these resonate with you, too?

Look at your list and ask yourself, 'Are these perceptions true? Are they facts?' Then, for each perception, write down three pieces of evidence that prove them not to be true.

Next, write down what the consequences are of keeping this perception. What is it costing you in your life? Make a conscious decision to give up the unwanted perception. Anything that comes after 'I am...' is a perception and shapes who you are. Imagine it like a piece of clothing you've always worn – it's time to take it off. You may feel a little naked without it, but trust me, you'll be free and soon wearing clothes that fit you much better.

Now, rewrite each false perception as a new one that you want. For example, 'I am not good enough' could become 'I love myself just as I am' or 'I am good enough.' 'I am too old' could become 'I am the perfect age to start my new business.' 'I am lazy' could become 'I enjoy being productive.' These perceptions will become your new identity – one that drives new actions and results in your life.

Here are some empowering perceptions to inspire you:

- **'I am decisive.'**
- **'I can do it.'**
- **'I am good enough.'**
- **'I am responsible.'**
- **'I am capable.'**
- **'I believe in myself.'**
- **'I have plenty of time.'**
- **'I am respected by others.'**
- **'I respect myself.'**
- **'I am productive.'**
- **'I am getting smarter every day.'**

This isn't positive thinking – it goes much deeper than that. You don't just say, 'I can do it'; that's just the start. You say it, commit to it, and *mean* it; you live from 'I can do it' and you act like you can. It becomes a new identity, a new you to show up in the world as.

What I'm about to share with you is the very essence and science behind starting before you're ready. According to self-perception theory, a well-established concept proposed by psychologist Daryl Bem, we form beliefs and perceptions about ourselves by observing our own behavior, especially when we're not sure about how we feel. You learn who you are by what you see yourself do. Therefore, the more you act with confidence, the more you start to believe you are confident.

As you act according to your chosen perceptions, your brain sees you doing it and starts to believe it's true. If you give an opinion in a meeting, you start to perceive yourself as a confident and assertive person. When you speak on stage, you start to perceive yourself as a public speaker.

You can change your self-perceptions with your actions. Your brain is like the audience and your behavior is the actor in the movie. Just as the audience forms an opinion of the character by what they see them do, the same is true for you. And as the director, you get to choose which roles you play. Starting before you're ready means playing the part until it becomes real. Act in alignment with your chosen perceptions for long enough and they'll become true.

If you want to have happiness, be happy.
If you want to have confidence, be confident.
If you want to have love, be love.

When you choose that you can, doors open, courses appear, mentors show up, and you get into action. If you perceive yourself as capable, not capable has to go. By changing the story you tell yourself, you can give yourself a new identity and live the life you want to live.

Your perceptions are not what you think but the space in which you think. See your perceptions as glasses that you've been wearing for a long time, clouding your decisions and limiting your choices. It's time to throw away the old perceptions and let them go. It's time to wear a new lens that gives you access to a new identity, new roles to play, and the most confident version of yourself. Anytime you notice yourself operating from an old perception, stop what you're doing, check in, and remind yourself of your new perceptions. Authenticity is being who you choose to be, and your perceptions are your choice to make.

As you choose your perception – 'I am enough,' 'I am courageous,' 'I am worthy,' 'I am valuable' – and come from this place, you will see it reflected back to you in the world around you. You don't have to wait until the future to have happiness, self-confidence, and love – you can be it now. We don't attract what we want; we attract who we are.

Take Ownership

What I'm about to share with you is one of the understandings that took me from feeling powerless to taking charge of my life and getting into action, and I know it can do the same for you.

When it comes to doing anything in your life, it's a choice, given the circumstances you have. You never 'have' to do anything; it might feel like it and, when it does, you feel powerless and it's impossible to tap into your confidence and inner authority from that place. If you feel like you *have* to go to work or you *have* to go shopping or you *have* to post on social media or you *have* to wake up early, life will feel like one big obligation, happening *to* you, and you're out of control. This makes you feel like a victim of life. When you *choose* to go to work – or anything else you're doing – you'll feel like you have ownership, you have a say in your choices and control in your reality.

Right now, it's 10 p.m. and I'm sitting writing the words you're reading. I could go to bed, but I am choosing to be here; I don't have to be. In the morning, I choose what time I wake or whether I set an alarm. When my kids wake, I choose to give them breakfast. You can't control what happens to you, but you can control how you respond. *Responsibility is your ability to respond.* I gave up my personal authority for years, giving away decisions and blaming myself and others, giving up my power. When I took it back, I took back my power. In any moment, you have the ability to choose your thoughts, attitude, and actions. You can take ownership of your perceptions and stories, not judging or blaming yourself, and take actions that align with your new stories. And actions are what create results.

- **The mindset of obligation:** Victim of life circumstances, driven externally by expectations, powerless.
- **The mindset of ownership:** In charge of your life, driven by choice and values, you're an authority and in control.
- **The energy of obligation:** Reactive, pressurized, and restrictive.
- **The energy of ownership:** Powerful, intentional, congruent.

Anytime you say, 'I have to,' replace it with, 'I choose to.' Remind yourself that it's a commitment you're choosing to make because it's what you'd rather do in that moment than take the other options. Many people say they 'have to' go to work, but the truth is they'd rather go to work than not go and get fired – it's still a choice given their circumstances. The circumstances of your life may not be your choice, but what you do with them is, and it's this choice that gives you your personal power and authority. 'I have to' drains your energy and makes you feel controlled by others, while 'I choose to' recharges your energy and puts you back in control. Bonus points if you say, 'I get to,' as this shifts you into a position of gratitude for choosing. Rather than 'I choose to cook dinner,' you can say, 'I get to cook dinner' and feel grateful for the opportunity – it will shift how you feel, connecting you with your inner feel good.

Take the initiative

Waiting for confidence means waiting to feel ready. One of the best ways to shatter this paradigm is to go first. When you take the initiative and go first, you show yourself that you can be a leader – you put into motion everything you have learned in this book. By not waiting, you give your brain evidence that you don't need to wait to feel ready. If you start a new job, go and introduce yourself to the manager at your first opportunity. If you go for lunch with a friend, offer to book the table or make some suggestions about where to go. If you're at an event and they ask for a volunteer to participate, put up your hand. Look for opportunities to take the lead by moving toward life rather than waiting or moving away from it.

Going first and taking the initiative will set you apart from most people and give your brain direct evidence that you're steering the ship, you're in charge, and you're confident – changing your self-perception. You'll also show yourself that you're willing to take up space, to not hide, to put yourself out there because you're worthy and valuable enough to do so. This will take you from being passive to proactive.

Awareness gives you choice

As we've seen, low self-confidence is the result of self-blame and buying into the limiting thoughts and self-perceptions you have. Awareness is like shining a light on the problem so you see it with clarity. When you believe all your thoughts to be true and are doubting yourself, it's because your awareness is lower. When you're more aware of your limiting thoughts as thoughts and not facts, you wake up to your true potential, and taking inspired action becomes easier.

The choices we have are limited or unlimited by our level of awareness – how conscious we are:

- **Level 1:** Life is happening to me – you have no choice and blame others for not starting. ('I don't have the time, money, or resources.')
- **Level 2:** Life is happening by me – you give up blame and take responsibility. ('I can make the time and money, and I can find the resources.')
- **Level 3:** Life is happening through me – you allow yourself to trust your inner wisdom and act from insight. ('I know I have plenty of time and take steps forward, trusting that the people and circumstances will arrive when I need them.')
- **Level 4:** Life is happening as me – you are one with life and fully free to embrace uncertainty without fear or resistance. You operate from flow, fully immersed in the present moment with nothing to prove and without the separation created by judgments. ('I am everything, which means money isn't separate from me, I am connected to it already; it's on its way.')

When awareness rises, you'll have understanding and compassion for yourself, and it's at this place that a powerful energy exists in you and courage becomes available again. You step out of fear and into clarity.

When you're aware of your limiting perceptions and see the truth – that they're not real – you can accept yourself more easily. When you're in flow and you lose yourself, this is when you're close to who you truly are. You'll find you're most confident when you're not thinking too much about yourself. You are the essence that experiences life. This means you're limitless because you can choose who you're being, and be it fully.

LENS CHECK

Take a moment to reflect on what life's like for someone who has total confidence and trust in themselves and their abilities. They give themselves permission to act and know they are guided by a higher power. How do they feel about themselves? How do they feel around others? They have courage and commitment in what they do and back themselves to do what they say they will. What do opportunities look like for them?

There's so much power in seeing you have the power. Choose to feel good about yourself. Choose your thoughts, choose your self-perceptions, choose to follow your promises with action, choose to accept yourself without conditions, and choose the results you want and go out and make them happen. Create this standard for yourself and live it.

Confidence in what you do comes from taking action, not from waiting for confidence. Confidence in who you are is already there. The paradox is that when you let go of trying to get it, you have it. Master not feeling ready yet, choosing your perspective, and taking action, and you'll be an expert at crossing the plank and walking the path of life. Now it's time to experience the rewards of courage, taking action, and starting before you're ready – it's time to finish strong.

KEY TAKEAWAYS

- **Stop waiting for confidence and get into action. Confidence in what you do will meet you on the other side of action.**
- **Remind yourself often that you are not your thoughts. Choose empowering thoughts about yourself, create your perception, and trust your inner wisdom.**
- **Take total responsibility for yourself, take ownership over your results and your life, and keep the promises you make to yourself, and you'll shift your self-perceptions and feel empowered to start – any time you choose.**

CHAPTER 10

Finish Great

You now have all the tools you need to get out of your head and into action. You've been taking bold steps, launching into the unknown, and starting, but there's one last area we need to address so you can reap the rewards of your new-found courage and confidence: the art of finishing. The finishing stages are where tensions are high, nerves rise, and fear can set in again.

Shipping your product, hitting 'post' and sharing a video with the world, completing a qualification, launching your website, or publishing your book are all acts of finishing. Finishing is saying, 'It's ready now' and following through with action, but, for so many of us, completing a task and moving on to the next feels impossible.

Maybe there's an idea inside of you – perhaps you got started and built the website, wrote the book, finished the painting, or have the product ready – but you haven't released it yet. If starting before you're ready is getting out of the gate, then finishing is closing it. So, what makes it so hard for us to close that gate?

The finishing stage is where all the blocks we've explored in this book get magnified to new levels. Self-doubt becomes self-destruction; impostor syndrome becomes full-on fraud; and perfectionism becomes aiming not for 100 percent but for 150 percent - a standard that doesn't even exist. As if placing our inner demons under a magnifying glass, everything becomes exaggerated and heightened, so it can feel impossible to finish. The reason? The moment you have to present a finished product to the world you open it up to critique. You might face criticism from others, but the real critic you have to deal with is, once again, the one inside your head. The truth is, sometimes it's going to go well - you finish and create success - and other times it won't go how you want it to - and your task in this final chapter is to master being OK with that.

Some of the world's finest products, services, and ideas are out there right now, hiding in people's heads, or in the Notes section of their phone, or on a scrap of paper in a drawer somewhere. There are many masterpieces made and never published, never released to the world as they're stuck in the ideas vault. The French artist Claude Monet was highly critical of his own work. Despite his immense talent, he destroyed many of his paintings, slashing up to 30 of them with a knife, as he didn't think they were good enough for public viewing. Many of the paintings he discarded were later considered masterpieces, including his *Water Lilies*. Leonardo da Vinci was reported to have continued to work on his famous painting the *Mona Lisa* for 11 years after he had actually 'finished' it. Whether it was Monet, Van Gogh, Da Vinci, or Michelangelo, many of the world's most respected artists kept unfinished work or didn't share it because they suffered with self-doubt – they didn't think it was good enough, even though the world would now consider what they created to be masterpieces.

> ## LENS CHECK
>
> Take a moment to reflect on what life's like for someone who fears finishing anything. How much do they get done? They attach their worth to their projects and want them to be perfect before sharing them with others. How do they feel about completing tasks? What thoughts do they have? What do they miss out on by never finishing?

There will always be more you could add, more you could research, more you could perfect. There are hundreds more chapters and words I'd love to add to this book, but at some point you have to say, 'It's ready' before you feel it is. You have to finish and put it out there and face the music or, just like many of those artists, you may die without the world getting the benefit of what you've created. You have art in you that we all need; you have ideas that will make the world better; and you have gifts to offer us all. Don't keep them in you – it's time to set them free.

In this final chapter, we'll explore some simple tools and tips to support you in finishing what you start and living a life of freedom, fortune, and fun.

Use the 80 Percent Rule

Trying to finish perfectly is not only impossible, it will slow down your progress and leave you feeling anxious. The 80 percent rule is a tool you can use to stop anxiety in its tracks. When you think you're 80 percent of the way to completion or you feel the task or project is 80 percent as good it can be, put it out there. This will save you trying to perfect it. Parkinson's Law states that our work expands to meet the time. This means that if you had two days or two weeks to complete a task, you would find more ways to perfect it to fill the time and, ultimately, something that you could finish in two days could end up taking you two weeks to complete. The 80 percent rule takes away the all-or-nothing nature of success and failure that you learned about in Chapter 1 and allows you to lean into the gray zone by getting used to doing slightly-less-than-perfect work. Don't be alarmed: Less than perfect doesn't mean failure; it means, once again, letting go of a need for perfect, which is an enemy of finishing.

At first, this may bring up some anxiety for you, but you can get used to this and break through. Often, when I put out a piece of work, post a video to social media, or send an email to a client, I have the feeling that more could be added, it might not be quite right, or it isn't good enough (good enough being perfect), and I smile and hit 'send' anyway. I don't let my thoughts determine my actions and you don't have to either. The 80 percent rule will help you meet more deadlines, finish more tasks, and get more done! You'll often find that if you have perfectionist tendencies, then your 80 percent perfect is someone else's 150 percent anyway.

There will always be more you can add

You can always add more to your work but remember this: The audience or the customer only needs so much. The extra things you think are needed may never have crossed people's minds. People don't know what you've left out and you can always save what you don't use now for other projects or ventures in the future.

Often, you can't know what you need until you finish it and put it out there. This is why many companies beta test products and launch without even having a product, because they want to avoid spending months making something no one wants.

Let Go to Let In

Starting and finishing are both part of one big continuum: infinity. Just like yin and yang, where two opposite forces complement each other, finishing is an important part of starting and starting is an important part of finishing. One without the other loses its significance. How satisfying would a football match be if there was no final whistle and score? How can you enjoy a painting that doesn't get finished? What would happen to a meal that doesn't get served? Starting marks the beginning of a cycle while finishing signifies the end, but they merge into each other. As dark fades there's light and as light fades there's dark.

Finishing is essential for change, adaptation, and progress. By finishing, you'll experience the satisfaction and sense of achievement that you would be robbed of if you didn't. Often you need to finish one task, project, or relationship in order to make space for the next. Much like a closed fist, you cannot grasp the next opportunity while holding on to the current one. This means letting go of attachment. Nothing lasts forever and developing the ability to let go is a powerful move.

Practice finishing often

One way to implement this in your life is to practice finishing often. Start with the little things so you build the habit and then progress on to bigger things. First, practice letting go of some items you no longer use. If you haven't worn an item of clothing in the past 12 months, or you have a book or a piece of furniture sitting there gathering dust, choose to give it away and notice any resistance you have. Do the same with an old habit or routine that no longer serves you, such as saying 'yes' automatically, or let go of an old rule you no longer want, such as 'I must always be approved of by others' (check back in with the tools in Chapter 8 if you need support with this!).

Next – and this is a great way to practice finishing – complete all the little tasks you start. If you have washing hanging up that's dry, don't just fold it and put it on the side, put it all away so the job is complete. If you start writing a text to a friend or an email to a colleague, finish it and press 'send.' Make your bed in the morning, not because it makes it tidy or because you 'have to,' but because you're completing the act of sleeping and starting the act of waking up. Do this for a week and then choose tasks that would benefit you if you completed them to keep up the habit.

Set deadlines

Another tip for developing the ability to let go is setting and hitting deadlines. Deadlines will force you to complete tasks and give up any of the perfectionistic tendencies we explored in Chapter 1 that cause you to try to avoid failure - such as doing endless research, over-preparing, avoiding discomfort, trying to make things perfect, and waiting to feel ready.

The mistake most people make is not setting deadlines because it causes them stress. Deadlines can make the outcome of your task or project seem more immediate, bringing your fears and the unknown into the present - fears of it not being good enough, failing, or judgment come to the forefront of your mind. However, as you now know, avoiding stress keeps many of the problems we've tackled in this book alive. Just because deadlines trigger stress, it doesn't mean you should avoid them, because they also offer you a breakthrough.

How do you feel after you hand in a project, finish an exam, or complete the task you started? While avoiding setting deadlines might give you a temporary sense of relief, it also prevents you from transforming the stress into success, experiencing the sense of achievement and the progress that comes from getting things done.

EXERCISE

Think of something you've started but haven't finished. Maybe it's an application for a new job, a video for social media, the final chapter of your book, or an email to potential clients to let them know you've set up your own business.

Now, set yourself a deadline for when you'll take that final step. Make it by the end of today or the end of the week – whatever feels appropriate. This deadline will act as a catalyst to get you out of your head and into action. It might bring up some doubts and anxiety, but it will also create excitement about making progress and achieving your goals. Think about how good it will feel when you meet the deadline.

Free Your Mind

Not only does finishing reduce your workload, clear your to-do list, and give you a sense of achievement, it also helps free up vital mental space and offer you more clarity due to a psychological phenomenon called the Zeigarnik effect. The Zeigarnik effect was discovered in the 1920s by a psychologist called Bluma Zeigarnik, following her work with her mentor and fellow psychologist, Kurt Lewin.[6] While in a café, Lewin and Zeigarnik noticed the server was able

6 Zeigarnik, B. (1927), 'Über das Behalten von erledigten und unerledigten Handlungen,' [On finished and unfinished tasks] *Psychologische Forschung*, 9: 1–85.

to remember the details of people's orders with astounding accuracy, even remembering what each individual customer had ordered and how much they owed. However, when the server was asked what the customers had ordered after they'd paid the bill and left, they couldn't recall the information. Puzzled, Lewin and Zeigarnik decided to investigate this further and came across a remarkable discovery: People remember and can recall incomplete and interrupted tasks better than the ones they've completed. Unfinished tasks create a state of tension, where the brain works hard to complete the task or close the unfinished loop. That tension keeps the task in the front of your mind as it's unfinished business, and this uses up mental energy and focus.

This explains why I couldn't stop watching the TV series *24*. Every episode ends with Jack Bauer in a situation you can't see him getting out of. I once stayed up until 6 a.m. to finish a series, which was on DVD at the time – so old school. The tension is created by the open loop and your brain wants to find out what it is and close the loop, whether you want to or not. You can use this effect to your advantage by keeping tasks open that you want to remember. I'll often leave a text unread if I want to remember to reply or leave a task open that I want to finish later that day.

However, finishing tasks frees up mental space in your mind because, when you complete tasks, they no longer sit in your mind taking up space and brain power. This allows you to focus on the next task you want to start or simply enjoy the present moment. Like getting closure from an ex who hurt you, the tasks disappear from your mind, they stop renting space for free, and you become free.

Close the loops by finishing and you'll gain confidence, clarity, and reduce mental clutter, and become a master of starting before you're ready – and finishing.

Don't expect perfection

As you use the tools in this book and experience freedom, you may begin to feel more yourself and maybe even invincible at times. I remember at one point thinking, *I've faced my fears and broken through my limiting beliefs; now I'm fully free*, and then it all came crashing down when self-doubt, procrastination, and fear inevitably came knocking again. The tools are only as good as when you use them and, at any point, your ego can have you come crashing down.

When the highs are high, be grateful for them and ground yourself, because there will be lows. Both highs and lows shall pass. There'll be times when you're not ready to start and that's OK. There'll be times when you think you've mastered it and your ego will taunt you with, 'You're not ready.' Lean into all of it, accept yourself, and don't let the inner or outer critics stop you from keeping on starting and finishing. Your successes and failures do not define you – remember, there can be no success without failure.

You Are Not Your Work

As the finishing line gets closer, you may hear the voice of your inner critic louder than ever before. At this stage of the game, it's vital to remember what we explored in Chapter 4: You have enough critics – don't be your own. You're not immune to fear and perfectionism, therefore you must bring awareness to your inner critic and compassion to yourself. One of the major blocks to finishing is attaching yourself to your work. It can feel like you *are* the painting, you *are* the book, or you *are* the business, but you're *not*. These things are an expression of you, they are a gift to the world, but you are not the gift itself.

The only thing that gets killed when you fail, the only thing that you risk damaging when you get judged, is your ego. Your ego is an idea of you, not the real you. So, when you have a chance to put something out into the world, you also have a chance to kill your ego, one little bit. It takes courage, trust, and self-love to take this leap. The fears you experience, the pressure and the self-doubt are all your ego attaching itself to what you do.

You are not your work in the same way I am not my T-shirt – it's something I wear, an expression of my fashion, but not me. My business is The Perception Coach and that's who I choose to show up as online – it's an expression of me, but it's not who I am, and it doesn't have to define me if I don't want it to. If the business fails, I don't fail and if the business dies, I don't die. I am the one creating it, I am not it. I can improve the coaching I provide and the services I offer without confusing them with me. This means I can criticize, challenge, and change what I do, without making it mean something about me – only my ego does that. I never have to judge myself or my work, even if others do. I wish this for all of you, to see that you are not your ego or your work.

You can be who you want to be and do what you love to do. You get to choose how hard you are on yourself and, if you're willing to be brave and release your work to the world and practice not judging yourself, you'll grow, learn, and evolve beyond your wildest dreams.

Be great, be bold, and stay humble.

To succeed with the fastest speed, most fun, and most freedom, you need to be willing to finish and, with experience, persistence, and self-compassion, you'll end up finishing great most of the time.

The Story of the Talking Parrot

This Sufi fable points us in the direction of escaping our limits and finding our personal freedom, and it's where I choose to finish this book and leave you to start the next chapter of your life's journey.

A merchant owned a talking parrot that was kept in a golden cage. The merchant loved the parrot and treated it well, but the parrot longed for freedom. One day, the merchant was preparing for a trip to the forest, and he asked the parrot if it wanted anything from its homeland. The parrot replied, 'Yes, please pass on a message to the parrots in the forest. Tell them that I'm very happy here, living in my cage and I miss them all dearly.' The merchant agreed and went on his journey. When he reached the forest, he found a group of wild talking parrots and he delivered his parrot's message to them. As soon as he finished, one of the wild parrots, with tears in its eyes, dropped dead and fell lifeless from the branch it was perched on. The merchant was shocked and puzzled by this.

When he returned home, he told his pet parrot about what had happened in the forest and, upon hearing the story, the pet parrot, with tears welling in his eyes, suddenly collapsed in its cage and hit the floor, dead. The merchant, heartbroken, opened the cage to remove the lifeless bird. At that very moment, the parrot sprang to life and flew to freedom, perching on the branch of a nearby tree. The merchant, confused and angered by what he'd just seen, remarked, 'You tricked me, why would you do that?'

The parrot replied to the merchant, 'The parrot in the forest sent me a very important message.'

'What did he say?' asked the merchant.

'He told me that if you want to escape from your cage, you must die while you're still alive.'

We are all caged by our past identities, and our ego likes to hold on to the idea of who we were. When taking steps on new ground, you won't feel ready – that's the old you wanting to stay in the cage of perceived safety and comfort. But the cage of the past will only continue to restrict you if you keep it alive by staying in it. As you start and finish before you're ready, you'll let go of the past you and fly out of the old cage, freeing yourself of your ego and any restrictions of your self-created identity. You will become free.

LENS CHECK

Take a moment to reflect on what life's like for someone who is a master at finishing things. They see life as an experiment and a chance to play and share their projects with the world. How do they view themselves? They've mastered all the tools in this book and enjoy completing projects and getting things done. What can they accomplish? How do they see the world? How do they feel? They see finishing as the key to unlock to their next adventure and they know that the end of each project adds to their self-confidence, experience, and wisdom.

Keep starting and finishing and remember that this journey never ends – it's a lifelong one and you're only just getting started. I wish you well, I stand by your side spiritually as you embark on the next steps of your journey, and I'll be there with love, cheering you on every step of the way.

Come back to this book when you need it but know that you have everything you need to take your next step, you always have. Be an inspired action-taker and, as always, big love.

KEY TAKEAWAYS

- **Let go of perfection and be willing to get your work out there when it feels 80 percent ready. This will stop your brain tricking you into never-ending perfectionism.**
- **Practice finishing tasks often so you get used to the feeling. You'll gain the satisfaction of completing tasks and that well-deserved sense of accomplishment.**
- **Remember, you are not what you do. This won't be your last chance; each time you finish something it's the start of something new - the journey is a lifelong one.**

Acknowledgments

There are many people that helped to make this book possible, but I must start with my parents. Both this book and I would not exist without you, and I appreciate you beyond words. I want to acknowledge the immense sacrifices you've made for me; only now, as a parent myself, can I begin to understand what those sacrifices mean. Thank you for your love and for encouraging me to follow my passions and pursue my dreams, which I am now living! You've always believed in me and allowed me to grow into someone I'm proud of, so thank you.

To my wife, Michelle, thank you for loving me unconditionally, and for being my own personal life coach. You're one of the strongest people I know mentally, spiritually, and emotionally. You're a master at starting before you're ready. Your support and love from day one has encouraged me to be the best version of myself. Thank you for holding the fort while I spent hundreds of hours in the office working on this project and for looking after our little ones at some of the most challenging of times. Thank you for being patient with me and for loving me throughout it all. You are a one-of-a-kind human.

Julia Kellaway, my editor extraordinaire. What a journey we've been on in such a short space of time. While I have much to learn, I feel like you've helped me rise up the levels of competence in writing much faster than I could have dreamed of. Your encouragement, honest feedback, and expertise have been invaluable, and I see how much of a genius you are at what you do. I appreciate how you've helped me find my writing style, organized these words, allowed me to get some of the most intangible ideas out of my head and onto paper, and challenged me to make this book and my writing the best it could possibly be. Thank you.

Thank you to all the amazing Hay House team. Thanks to Helen Rochester for getting me started on this journey and lighting the sparks for this book in its early stages. Thank you to Emma Hill for your amazing work editing the book in the final stages, for your sharp eye picking up anything I had missed or that didn't fit, and for helping the ideas and tools flow in the best possible way. Thanks to Grace Rahman for your ongoing support and expertise to make this book read, look, and feel aligned with the message and for bringing my ideas to life. Thank you to Michelle Pilley for welcoming me into the Hay House family, which has been a dream come true. Thanks to Reid Tracy and Kelly Notaras for your wisdom in the valuable Authorpreneur community. Thanks to Kezia Bayard-White for walking me along this journey and helping me over the finish line. Special thanks also to Jo Burgess, Katherine O'Brien, Portia Allen-Chauhan, Nina Hayes-Thompson, Tom Cole, Anthony Bird, Alexandra Gruebler, and Lucy Buckroyd.

Thank you to my amazing clients for teaching me about life and what it means to be human. For each person who has sat with me face to face and trusted me to hold space for you to dream big, face your fears, and be open to my challenges, I appreciate you. It's a privilege to support you along your journeys and I've learned more from each of you than I would from any textbook. The depth of your wisdom is what shapes my perspective and the depth of what I offer in this book is owed to each of you.

Thank you to my friends and family for being my biggest supporters. To my sister, for always being there for me. To my children, for loving me unconditionally, helping me expand, and for many of the lessons shared in these pages. You teach me what it means to be your full authentic self, be messy, and start badly. For my Nan, who taught me immense kindness, and Pop, who taught me to live life to the full. To Mikey Harris, for helping me change the lens on my perception when I needed to. Thank you Bircan Tulga, for your friendship, support, and behind-the-scenes camera expertise. You are a true master at capturing the perfect moment.

To the friends and family who I've not named as there are too many to mention – you know who you are, so please hear these words about you. Thank you for supporting my growth over the years, for celebrating with me when I succeeded, and seeing the greatness in me when I've been climbing the mountain. Your love and words of encouragement have helped me to see what's possible and each of you has offered me a mirror to myself, which has contributed to the life lessons I share in these pages.

To all my supporters and audience, thank you to every one of you who has followed my journey, watched, liked, and commented on my videos and posts over the years. Hearing about how these have lifted your mood, shifted your perspective, or changed your life has been a great source of motivation to keep me inspired along the way. This book is for you, a tool to help you on your journey into inspired action and the life you want. Without your continued support and love, I wouldn't have got to this stage of my journey and a book would not have been possible. I appreciate every one of you who I've connected with and look forward to meeting many more of you in the future.

To Hunter Fogarty, what can I say my brother; thank you for your wisdom and friendship over the years, you are wise beyond your years. Thank you for teaching me how to grow an audience online to share my message with and for seeing something in me at the very start of my journey. This book would not have been published without you planting the idea of publication in my head and I'm so grateful you did. Thank you for challenging me to start this book before I was ready.

Chris Finn, thanks for helping me grow as a coach and human being. Our personal $20k agreement to challenge each other's limitations and call each other 'up' has expanded the way I think, much of which has contributed to this book.

Thank you to Sarah Anderson CBE, Terence Collis, and all the team at The Listening Place who made me feel welcome, helped me learn non-judgment and kindness, and taught me how to support others. You're amazing people and the work you do is valuable and so important.

I've worked with many exceptional coaches, teachers, and trainers over the years who have helped me expand my perceptions. Special thanks to Ryan Mathie, Maxwell Nee, Frankie Cote, Alex Manzi, and Sachin Sharma. I'd like to thank my mentor Lyndsay Brady for teaching me on the deepest level how our perceptions drive our actions and Mark Howard for teaching me that when you find the good feeling in you, you will have all the answers you need. Thank you to everyone at Toastmasters, Amanda Zwarts, and all the team for helping me grow my confidence while speaking and growing personally – it's an amazing environment for personal growth.

Finally, I want to acknowledge all those I have been inspired by and who've helped upgrade my thinking at a distance, including but not limited to: Wayne Dyer, Tony Robbins, Albert Ellis, Mel Robbins, Brené Brown, Les Brown, Earl Nightingale, Alan Watts, Neville Goddard, Susan Jeffers, Viktor Frankl, Frederick Dodson, and Eckhart Tolle. I'm grateful for your contributions and that each of you never gave up on your dreams so you could inspire me to follow mine.

© Bircan Tulga, Black Edge Studios

About the Author

Jon Prince is a former professional poker player turned fully accredited coach, speaker, and author. As the founder of The Perception Coach, Jon works with people from all walks of life, all over the world, including in the UK, America, Canada, Australia, and across Europe. His clients include influencers, high roller poker players, CEOs, business owners, life coaches, and an AFL Superstar. Jon's mission is to help people discover who they are, reach their full potential, and create the life they really want.

@theperceptioncoach

www.theperceptioncoach.com

We hope you enjoyed this Hay House book. If you'd like to receive our online catalog featuring additional information on Hay House books and products, or if you'd like to find out more about the Hay Foundation, please contact:

Hay House Publishers (India) Pvt Ltd
Muskaan Complex, Plot No. 3,
B-2, Vasant Kunj, New Delhi 110 070
Phone: +91 11 41761620
www.hayhouse.co.in

—

Published in the United States by:
Hay House LLC, P.O. Box 5100, Carlsbad, CA 92018-5100
(760) 31-7695 or (800) 654-5126
www.hayhouse.com® • www.hayfoundation.org

Published in Australia by:
Hay House Australia Publishing Pty Ltd
18/36 Ralph St., Alexandria NSW 2015
Phone: +61 (02) 9669 4299
www.hayhouse.com.au

Published in the United Kingdom by:
Hay House UK Ltd
1st Floor, Crawford Corner,
91–93 Baker Street, London W1U 6QQ
Phone: +44 (0)20 3927 7290
www.hayhouse.co.uk

—

'The gateways to wisdom and knowledge are always open.'

Louise Hay